To maggie,
with love and blessings
on your way.

Song of the Self

Song of the Self

Biblical Spirituality and Human Holiness

Carol Ochs

Trinity Press International

Valley Forge, PA

First Edition 1994

Trinity Press International
P.O. Box 851
Valley Forge, PA 19482-0851

Cover design by Jim Gerhard

The poem "Could Be" (pp. 17–18) is reprinted from *Kodachromes in Rhyme* by Ernesto Galarza, © 1983 by University of Notre Dame Press. Used by permission.

Library of Congress Cataloging-in-Publication Data

Ochs, Carol.
    Song of the self : biblical spritiuality and human holiness / by Carol Ochs. — 1st ed.
        p. cm.
    Includes bibliographical references and index.
    ISBN 1-56338-096-X:
    1. Bible. O.T. Genesis—Criticism, interpretation, etc.
    2. Bible. O.T. Job—Criticism, interpretation, etc. 3. Self—
    Biblical teaching. I. Title.
    BS1235.2.O24   1994
    248—dc20
                                                            94-4924
                                                            CIP

94 95 96 97 98 6 5 4 3 2 1
Printed in the United States of America.

*To Clara Michaels Blumenthal
who enthusiastically embraces life*

Contents

Acknowledgments

I am grateful to the students in my metaphysics class at Simmons College, who allowed me to test out my ideas, and to the Simmons Fund for Research, for a grant to input data. My warmest thanks to the Reverend Robert Bilheimer, Padraic O'Hare, and Pamela Lloyd, who generously gave of their time to read the manuscript, offered helpful suggestions, and provided encouragement, and to Michael Ochs, who lent his support and his editing skills.

Introduction

I don't know who I am. That would not be remarkable, except that I am at a stage in life when I might be expected to know: in my mid-fifties, married for more than thirty years, the mother of two adult daughters, a teacher at the same institution for twenty-five years, and a resident in the same house for twenty years. But increasingly I am aware that none of these facts points to the mystery of who I am. I don't know how the particulars of my life's history relate to my essential identity. What is the significance of my living in the second half of the twentieth century? Or in the Western Hemisphere? Or as a member of my particular family?

I know that I am not simply all I have experienced, or the sum of my relationships, or my work, or my national origin. All of these are factors, but they miss the heart of the question because I am not trying to explain myself to someone else, I am trying to explain myself to me.

I have come to realize that the Hebrew scriptures repeatedly show us and tell us who we are. When I first turned to the Bible, I focused on what it says about the nature of God and about our relationship to God. But as I became more comfortable with the text and more familiar with the characters, I realized that the Bible says even more about my own nature. By entering into the biblical stories, I found that the Bible did not present a doctrine about who I am, but that it initiated, instead, a process by which I could transform and claim my self.

The starting point in my quest for the self proved to be the texts of the Hebrew scriptures. Not all the texts were equally valuable in my search. I identified primarily with the stories of Genesis: the expulsion from Eden, Cain's slaying of Abel, the

1

Flood, God's call to Abraham, and Abraham's descendants working out their family relationships. After Genesis, the biblical focus turns from paradigmatic individuals to the fortunes of an entire people. The Book of Exodus, which recounts the Israelites' journey into freedom, aided me greatly in my quest. And finally, I found the Book of Job central to my self-understanding. Job seeks to find the meaning of his self's very existence in the face of loss, suffering, and tragedy. My own questions arose at a time in my life when the assumptions and structures that had supported my self were suddenly thrown into doubt and my earlier answers no longer satisfied me.

I am not alone in using the Bible as a way of naming the central experiences in my life—these texts have helped people form their self-understanding for four thousand years. Even when I disagree with the texts and want to challenge them, I do so in terms of categories formulated in the scriptures themselves. I approach the texts with a sense of engagement: these are not dead artifacts to be reverently preserved, but living arguments, to be accepted or challenged, that have current implications for the way I live. I bring all that I have known and experienced to my struggle with the texts and allow them to challenge every aspect of my life. Out of this encounter with the Hebrew scriptures comes the experience of revelation, not as a tradition handed down, but as a first-person experience wrested from grappling with the texts.

I have read the Bible as a repeated account of courtship, as God woos all of us into a deeper and deeper intimacy. I have also read it as one slow, infinitely patient courtship pursued over millennia, with the narrative events from Abraham to Job detailing the many different ways God participates in the separate parts of Creation. In this view, Abraham is seen as an early manifestation of a self that is later portrayed by Job in a more developed form. And I have read the stories as showing the self "writ large," a working out of God's relationship to the people. With each reading I discovered the self, with its awakenings and longings, its resistance and defensiveness, and behind it all I began to see an ever-patient God calling me to my authentic being.

The Bible gives a way to name and think about experiences that are otherwise inexpressible. I have repeatedly used the biblical texts to help me form my unformed thoughts and give voice to the inarticulate. It is this use of the Bible that I invite readers to try as, together, we search for the self.

In attempting to share this quest, I will start from the position that we don't know who we are, and that coming to know who we are is the central concern of religion. When the Delphic Oracle says that our task is to "know thyself" and adds the line, not usually included, "and thou shalt know God," we need not conclude that the self *is* God, but merely that knowing who the self is can keep us from projecting it onto our conception of God. Just as knowing our own visual limitations allows us to compensate when trying to see what a scene is in itself and not merely how it looks to us, so knowing our self can allow us to perceive reality as it is, rather than reality as it is for us. The world view expressed in the Hebrew scriptures, which differs significantly from that of the Greeks, still shares with it the sense that knowing the self is the central concern of true religious practice.

One way to begin to give expression to our own confusion, to articulate it and to explore its implications, is to see the way that confusion is formulated in Genesis. We will look at the Creation accounts and seek to represent the discomfort that sets us on our quest for the self. We begin with Eden and the expulsion from Eden, and trace how self and otherness are worked out in Genesis.

The Bible is written in narrative form. Our lives as well can be understood in narrative form. Each of us experiences plot development, climax, and denouement. The modern theological view of the "narrative quality of experience" is essentially correct. The earliest narratives of which we have any record were sung. I will suggest that song is prior even to narration, and that there is a musical ordering to our own consciousness. We will see that music, even without being linked to a text, plays an essential structural role in our consciousness. Through the Song at the Sea in Exodus, we will discover the musical quality of experience and draw out the role of an aesthetic principle in our understanding of reality.

The fundamental tool we will use in our quest for the self is the distinction between appearance and reality. This distinction is drawn in radically different ways in the biblical and Platonic world views. The biblical view affirms the reality of time, change, multiplicity, and the material world, all of which are regarded as less than real in the Greek philosophical world view. As people raised with a Western consciousness, we need to sort out which aspects of the distinction between appearance and reality come to us from our Greek philosophic heritage and which aspects are biblical. We will see that it is a commitment to time and the changes that time can bring that allows for the prophetic consciousness and the call for social justice.

Memory is central to our understanding of self. But memory is neither passive recall nor is it value-free. There are many different ways of remembering what has happened to us. The Bible illustrates the positive formation of a shared memory for the Children of Israel and how that reconstructed memory can strengthen us during times of trial.

Wandering in the desert was the single most formative experience for the Children of Israel. Studying how that experience worked for them will enable us to explore the metaphoric deserts we must face in coming to know and accept our self. The components of this desert include not only fear, vulnerability, aggression, and terror, but also the source of creativity and revelation.

Central to any understanding of our self is the awareness that it is in process, moving on a trajectory from childhood, through youth and adulthood, and into old age. The process of aging provides a fertile area for examining the revelation inherent in the normal life cycle. Aging tells us which aspects of the self are enduring and essential. The insights inherent in aging are central to a religion teaching that revelation occurs in and through time. In examining the implications of aging, we can also raise the question of whether any aspect of the self survives death.

Some philosophies and some interpretations of Eastern religions have declared that space, time, and the "other" factors central to the self's shaping are unreal. This view will be explored from the biblical perspective and then rejected. We will then return to Genesis and consider a new reading of the important text dealing with the Tree of the Knowledge of Good and Evil.

Our quest for the self must contend with the inevitable losses and lettings-go that form an essential part of the life process. We must try to discover if coming into greater intimacy with God necessarily entails leaving much behind.

Finally, we need to draw out the conclusions inherent in all that we examine. In the process of trying to understand the self, the very self that we search for is transformed, and the fundamental questions we raise are also transformed. The question we will finally answer is not the one we raise at the beginning.

1 | *Genesis*

The questions that lead us to reexplore our identity arise because of specific events that we encounter or experience. For example, illness may cause us to reevaluate how we view the relationship of the mind to the body, a loss of status may challenge our sense of identity, or a breakdown in the family structure may lead us to question our place in the world. The self requires our reexamination when the way we understand it no longer functions for us. Aging frequently stimulates such reexamination because through time, and the revelation inherent in its passing, we discover that our answers are inadequate.

A quest for the self always bring us back to our origins, spiritually as well as psychologically. When we examine our origins the second time around, we concern ourselves less with unresolved issues of blame or judgment in our family drama and more with understanding our identity. Even after we have learned all that we can about our parents, we still find ourselves in a position similar to the one represented by the Zen koan: "What was your original face before your parents were born?" We know that we are more than the mere products of our parents, and that understanding our parents is necessary but not entirely sufficient for understanding who we are.

Our quest for the self takes us beyond our parents and opens us to the larger Creation of which they and we are a part. In opening up to Creation we must also be open to examining our own creativity. We were not simply created, we seem to be co-creators in forming and transforming our self.

We can begin to think about these issues by reviewing the

opening chapter of Genesis, which describes the creative process and the early days of Creation. Genesis 1 shows us, first of all, that we are not self-caused. We know that, of course, but even though we recognize our dependence in coming into being, we fall back into a self-knowledge that requires us to be self-made and self-sufficient. In reflecting on this opening chapter, we conclude that a final understanding of our self must take into account that we were called into being. Our meaning, then, will be bound up with the larger Creation with which we were called into being and of which we are a part, and with the Creator who has called us forth. Self-understanding that derives from the larger Creation does not depend on socially constructed definitions. We are more than the many roles we have played in our lives. The self freed from its social moorings may well be a mystery.

The mysterious aspect of the self compels us to remember that Genesis 1 relates the story of a creation, not an illusion. Any understanding of the self must take that self and all the rest of creation seriously. Some philosophies regard the self as illusory. Salvation within those traditions comes when believers recognize the unreal aspects of all creations. Biblical religion, while finding that we can misunderstand and misname our self, never considers the self to be an illusion, or a temporary veil to be discarded. Because many of the world's peoples are taught to think of the self as unreal, and because we become frustrated in trying to grasp the elusive nature of the self, we might be tempted to discard the whole notion of self. But however problematic and mysterious it may be, the self we want to uncover is not an illusion but a product of God's deliberate creation. Through this problematic self, we interact with others, make our contribution to this world, and come to know God. In the transformative process of contemplation, we can have experiences in which we are no longer conscious of the self. Such episodes do not negate the self's reality or existence. We need to remember that experiences come unnamed, and we should avoid rushing to name them within a particular system.

The Creation account offers us an important starting point in our quest for the self because it informs us about the context within which we were created, a context that precedes social structures. In Genesis 1:3 God says, "Let there be light." For many, then, the first creation is light. But in Isaiah 45:7 God states,"I form the light, and create darkness." Is darkness merely the absence of light, or does it have an existence of its own? Behind this question lies a concern raised in Isaiah, further on in the same sentence, where God states, "I make peace, and create evil." Our quest for the self may compel us to face discomforting questions about our understanding of evil. Darkness is not evil, it is the opposite of light; evil is the opposite of peace. Juxtaposing these pairs of opposites disturbs our usual way of construing reality. And while we may have heard of the "coincidence of opposites," it is an idea reserved for mystics and does not seem to assist us in our quest for self-understanding. Yet the coincidence of opposites remains as an issue to be addressed—a biblical clue about our ultimate identity that dates from the first day of Creation and precedes our own entrance into the universe.

Day One of Creation raises enough issues to make us question whether this approach will really prove helpful, but let us look further. Creation in Genesis continues by distinction and division, by separation and naming, and by a call for creatures to be fruitful and to multiply. Distinction, division, and separation remind us that we are finite, limited by the many different things that surround us, and in our creation as male and female we are simultaneously limited and completed by relationship. This is the context in which we are called into being.

We must look more fully at our own creation. According to Genesis, we are created in the image of God. That statement contains both promise and warning: it promises us an identity that is worth the quest, and it warns us not to reduce the self to any collection of roles, relationships, history, characteristics, or traits. At the core of the self is inexhaustible mystery. This is both reassuring, as our roles change and our status drops away, and frightening, as we enter into uncharted ways.

We are created in God's image, and we are created in relationship. In the first account of Creation we are created simultaneously male and female, and in the more protracted account in Genesis 2 we are created separately for one another. In either case our very identity seems to require the other that mirrors, complements, and completes us. We probably cannot be fully "I" until there is the other whom we can love.

However challenging the first two chapters of Genesis might be, they still deal only with the self and its context. When we read on, however, we are confronted not only with the other that complements and completes us, but with the other that challenges and threatens us. If we ponder how the serpent came to the Garden, we must conclude that God placed it there, just as God placed there Adam and Eve and all the animals and plants. At the end of the six days of Creation, "God saw all that He had made, and found it very good" (Gen. 1:31). How can God affirm the goodness of Creation when the serpent lurks in the garden? We are accustomed to thinking of the serpent as a villain, but we should really think of it as a creation of God.

We think of the Edenic state as a time of unity and utter simplicity. The distinctions and oppositions that fill our lives are seemingly absent in Eden. A first reading of the text tends to support this view: "A river issues from Eden to water the garden, and it then divides and becomes four branches" (Gen. 2:10) tells us that a river that is single in Eden branches out beyond the Garden's borders to become four rivers—unity becomes multiplicity. The forbidden fruit of the Tree of the Knowledge of Good and Evil, whose presence seems anomalous in Eden, represents the knowledge of distinction formulated in a dualistic manner (good *versus* evil). But a more careful reading of the text contradicts the assumption that Eden is a state of simplicity. Duality does not originate with the Tree; in fact, distinction, duality, and multiplicity precede Adam and Eve's creation, as a quick rereading of Genesis 1 shows. The real problem represented by the Tree is not that eating its fruit taught us something new, but that the serpent so focuses us on duality that we lose sight of the underlying unity. When we age, we need bifocal eyeglasses. One sort of bifocal vision—seeing both duality and deeper unity at the same time— opens us to the context in which we have been set down and the awareness of the Creator in and within the creation. In normal vision we need two eyes, not merely to have a fallback in case one of them is injured, but to experience perspective and depth. Analogously, our capacity to recognize both difference and underlying unity allows us to experience perspective and depth. We need both kinds of vision.

If the serpent seduces us into emphasizing duality, the biblical text also offers a corrective vision by inviting us back to rediscover unity. The Hebrew scriptures lead to a unity of vision by five paths: (1) exploring and collapsing all dualisms; (2) abolishing simple discrimination and difference; (3) showing how an individual life is challenged over time and how in one life we are called to encompass several people; (4) demonstrating that life over time is tempered, if we consider the entire text from Abraham to Job as encompassing a single life; and (5) reminding us repeatedly that God is the cause of both good and evil.

Collapsing Dualisms

The most important statement of faith that exists in Judaism is the prayer *Shema:* "Hear, O Israel! the Lord our God, the Lord is One" (Deut. 6:4). The unity expressed in this central doctrine is not simply quantitative (there is one God, rather than two or three), but qualitative. As we reflect on this creed, we come to feel the wholeness of the universe and the interconnection between everything it contains. On one level we may have always sensed this unity and relatedness, but it is difficult to accept intellectually. While we know that things cannot be absolutely other and still share the same universe, emotionally we tend to remain dualistic. Perhaps we are mind-body dualists because our bodies make us ill at ease, or we affirm the absolute distinction between good and evil because we are judgmental. And surely life is opposed to death, or else why bury the dead? But over time we see these dualisms break down. We come to know that the body is the physical expression of the mind. We come to see how closely good and evil resemble one another (which is why morality poses such difficult questions). And we learn that death, like aging, is not something outside that comes to get us, but a stage of the self: just as there is our older self, there is our dead self. We begin to recognize that our challenge lies in becoming aware of the self that can live through its own death.

But the *Shema* does not end with the statement "the Lord is One"; it continues, "And thou shalt love the Lord thy God with all thy heart, and with all thy soul, and with all thy might" (Deut. 6:5). Love plays a critical role in our coming to recognize completely the oneness of God.

We experience, from time to time, the omnipresence of love. If the statement "everything is love" is to be more than a sigh, we must add that we find meaning in all that occurs, that we will cooperate with that meaning, and that we understand that the meaning is fed not only by what we desire (which we name good), but also by what thwarts our desire (which we name evil); both further the meaning to which we assent.

When evil and good both become occasions of love, we can realize experientially and accept cognitively that distinctions are provisional and methodological but not final and absolute. Dualisms arise and, on inspection, break down. The great builder of dualisms is fear: fear cries out for boundaries, divisions, distinctions, and absolutes, but love casts out fear.

The formula for breaking down dualisms sounds simple, yet its effect is something like an earthquake. We see this more clearly when we look at a fundamental dualism, creation and destruction, and see how it relates to our quest for the self. Like all dualisms, that of creation and destruction is based on a distinction that is plausible, even obvious. But a careful examination of creation shows that it entails destruction—the two processes are merely different perspectives on a single process. The essential dualism of self and other, the starting point for all other dualisms, is itself transformed in the process of creating/destroying the self. Let us look at aging in this context. The aging process can be viewed as creating the self or destroying it, or it can be regarded as an agent of the self's creation that eventually becomes the agent for its destruction. In the aging process we discover that even within our selves we carry the other, the other of our earlier self. The implications of aging will be discussed further in chapter 6.

The Hebrew scriptures provide us with a major text for examining the breakdown of all dualisms. Genesis 1 shows the relationship of creation to destruction: to create something new is to destroy its earlier form. Whoever resists the new experiences transformation as destructive. The narratives of the Patriarchs show the interrelationship of self and other: the Patriarchs' cycle of stories is an extended meditation on the relationship of father to son, wife to concubine, brother to brother, and sister to sister. Texts in Deuteronomy, Lamentations, Job, and Isaiah show the connections between good and evil: in each of these texts God is said to be the source of both what we desire and what thwarts our desire.

Abolishing Simple Differences

The process of breaking down dualisms is played out slowly through the Hebrew scriptures. The Egyptians' drowning at the Red Sea causes us unease. According to the Talmud (Megillah 10b), God tells the angels to stop singing because "my children are drowning." The Bible recognizes that both Jews and Egyptians are God's children. The tension of opposites is played out even more strongly in Psalm 136, with its repeated refrain that "[God's] steadfast love is eternal." Although verse after verse declares God's steadfast love, God "drowned Pharaoh and his host in the Red Sea." Then the refrain, "His steadfast love is eternal," sticks in the throat. The psalm works like a dialogue of Plato, in which an apparent discrepancy helps bring us to a deeper level of meaning.

The first part of the psalm portrays the God of all creation, not the parochial God of a particular people with its individual national interests. The God of the opening lines of Psalm 136 is "Supreme God," "Lord of lords," "who alone does great wonders." The goodness of God is exemplified by God's creation of the heavens and the spreading of the earth over the waters. The specific gifts to humanity mentioned in this psalm are the great lights—the sun to dominate the day and the moon and stars to dominate the night. This universal perspective challenges the narrow interests of the remaining part of the psalm. The sun, moon, and stars do not shine for any one group of people: all of God's creation is illuminated by these gifts. So even while the Children of Israel discover God in and through the unique events of their own history, the God they discover is the God of all creation.

Challenge over a Single Lifetime

The first portrait of aging and the tempering that time works upon character may be found in the story of Jacob (Genesis 25ff).[1] Jacob already causes anguish to his mother *in utero,* proves himself to be feisty at birth, and remains devious through young adulthood. Then a physical disability marks a spiritual transformation (Genesis 32), a change we can also note in some of our contemporaries. Later we see Jacob reduced from primary actor in the biblical drama to impotent suffering elder, left bereft as his sons conspire against their brother Joseph. We then see him at a later stage as he goes down to Egypt after experiencing another vision of God. And finally we witness his remarkable perspective and clarity of vision as he pronounces his deathbed testament. Genesis portrays the transformations of aging so successfully because it regards time as a medium of both revelation and change, and it focuses on time's unidirectional nature. When we recognize that time is a medium of transformation, we see that we play many different roles within a single lifetime. One simple character assignment as villain, hero, fool, or victim will not do—Jacob manages to be all of these in the course of a long eventful life.

Tempering over Generations

In addition to showing how time tempers the course of an individual life, the Hebrew scriptures show that growth and transformations occur over the course of generations. Let us assume for a moment that the many characters in Genesis are merely different aspects of a single life, in fact, that our own lives are being played out in the stories not only of Abraham, Sarah, Isaac, Rebecca, Jacob, Rachel, and Leah, but in all the characters, major and minor.

We are Isaac, whose role is that of keeping the faith, not of innovating in the ways of his father Abraham or the aggressive ways of his son Jacob. But Isaac is also the first biblical character to love. When he tries to pass off his wife as his sister (as Abraham had also done), his ruse is discovered because he treats her fondly. And Isaac is the first to mourn: he finds some comfort after the death of his mother only when Rebecca is brought to him. Ishmael joins Isaac for Abraham's burial, suggesting that Isaac had somehow kept in touch with his exiled older brother. So in Isaac we find someone of feeling and compassion.

We are also Esau, who from the perspective of our tradition—which is that of his brother Jacob—is not an appealing character. But Esau, viewed without the tales that have surrounded him, is someone we must claim as part of ourselves. When Jacob's son Joseph meets his brothers in Egypt, he explains their having sold him into slavery with the words, "You meant evil against me, but God meant it for good" (Gen. 50:19). When Esau is reunited with Jacob, Esau can kiss his brother because he, too, recognizes that while Jacob meant the stealing of their father's blessing for evil, God meant it for good. Jacob may have meant to cheat Esau out of God's blessing, but God's blessing cannot be stolen: whoever is blessed by God is blessed. Esau, looking over the twenty years since Jacob fled to Haran, could recognize that he had been deeply blessed. He had fathered a dozen children, he possessed large herds of cattle, and best of all, he felt free of any bitterness toward Jacob and any desire for revenge.

Can Jacob really recognize and identify with Esau? A prior question would have to be, Who is Esau? Jacob had never asked himself that, not when he bought his birthright and not when he stole his brother's blessing. But when he saw Esau after a twenty-year separation, Jacob said, "To see your face is like seeing the face of God" (Gen. 33:10). We might attribute his saying that to the same wily ways that Jacob has used all his life, such as sending herds to Esau as a bribe to assuage his brother's presumed anger. But Jacob's statement follows a night of wrestling with an angel, an experience that leaves him transformed in body (he has developed a limp) and in character (he is no longer arrogant). In telling Esau that seeing him was like seeing the face of God, Jacob means that having wrestled throughout the night with his deepest fears he could now see his brother free of all the attributes that he had projected onto him throughout their childhood. But there is something even more redeeming in this vision. When I recognize that my most fearsome enemy is not my brother but myself, and that I have confronted and wrestled with this self all night, I can greet my brother as a herald that my enemies—that is, my fears—will be overcome.

If we are Esau, are we also the Egyptians? Yes: we have not only been enslaved, but we have also enslaved others. God's blessing allows us to recognize the ways in which we enslave others so that we may release them with gifts. The signs (in the form of plagues) that Moses brings to Pharaoh as well as to the Children of Israel are not merely threats, they are a form of revelation that releases at least some of the Egyptians from the role of oppressor as they come to know God.

If we are all these people, then what is the meaning of chosenness, of trying to be this rather than that, and of covenant? We cannot become our authentic self—the person we are meant to be—by suppressing our identification with other people, but we need focus and direction. Covenant provides us with both, and also enables us to become our authentic self. Covenant is not a reward, it is a process that transforms our multifaceted self into one that is unified around a relationship to God. We do not achieve this self by slaying the Egyptians, cheating Esau, or casting out Hagar, nor do we achieve it in competition with others. God, unlike Jacob, does not play favorites. We achieve our authentic self by loving God.

Of course we are chosen, and it is irrelevant that God chooses all peoples. What matters is that we are loved, that we have been loved, and that our continuing awareness of this love transforms us. We decide to remember that we are chosen, and we choose to shape our lives around that commitment.

When Job is shown God's love and concern for Leviathan, Behemoth, and the ostrich, Job's question about the meaning of evil is answered only if his sense of self has expanded to include all of God's creation. The self that is constricted to mean "me, not you" or "we, not them" is always at risk and in need of defense. But the self that expands to include not only the Children of Israel but the Egyptians as well can stretch out, relax, and be loved by God.

An awareness that we live out the experiences and insights of all of the biblical characters breaks down the fundamental dualism of *me* and *you,* or *self* and *other.* It also reinforces our sense that time plays a role in our transformation. The expanded concern and appreciation for creation that allows Job to recant differs markedly from the concern for immediate progeny that preoccupies Abraham, Isaac, and Jacob.

God Is the Cause of Both Good and Evil

The notion that both blessings and curses have their source in God is the essential teaching of a poem in which Moses quotes God:

> See, then, that I, I am He;
> There is no god beside Me.
> I deal death and give life;
> I wounded and I will heal.
> (Deut. 32:39)

This teaching is found as well in Isaiah's troubling statement, "I am the Lord, and there is none else; I form the light, and create darkness; I make peace, and create evil" (Isa. 45:7). The same doctrine occurs in Lamentations: "Whose decree was ever fulfilled, / Unless the Lord willed it? / Is it not at the word of the Most High/That weal and woe befall?" (Lam. 3:37–38). This faith that God is the one source of all that exists—blessings as well as curses, good as well as evil—lies at the heart of the *Shema.* "The Lord is One" means that there is a single source for all that we experience in this world. Theoretically we acknowledge that there is only one source for all that is; emotionally we find it difficult to recognize God as the source of curses as well as blessings.

We are created in the image of God, carrying within ourselves a multiplicity of forces. We project our own divided lives onto external reality. Just as we can trace all things back to their source in the one God, so can we unify the opposing forces that we experience in our own lives. When we accept the unity of our lives, we will see the unity around us. Once we realize that we are strong and independent, yet also vulnerable, dependent, and needy, then we can reconcile the opposites we find in the outside world. As we accept ourselves more fully, we become aware that in the world of one God, opposites are reconciled.

In the Hebrew scriptures evil is never confused with good, but neither is it destroyed: it becomes transformed and reconciled. Without losing our capacity to discriminate, we recognize that nothing is absolutely separated from anything else and that every creature contains within it an aspect that is redeemable.

The Hebrew scriptures offer these five ways of rediscovering unity to counterbalance the Tree's dualistic fruit. Our quest for the self requires us to recognize and claim the unity underlying the multiplicity that eating the fruit opens up for us.

From the timeless and placeless Eden, we enter into historical time and particular place, and we take on individual identities. Our distinctiveness, which is not simply our "fallen" condition, plays a genuine role, if not an ultimate one. Historical time is linear, or unidirectional: things happen once, and their consequences are irrevocable. These unique events determine our individuality, or uniqueness. As we enter into historical time, the concepts of causality and responsibility come to the fore. Our nonillusory self is shaped by the nonillusory time within which it acts.

In Eden, we begin with the undifferentiated self, which cannot distinguish itself from others. Only after eating the fruit can Adam and Eve recognize one another's nakedness. There is some initial differentiation—Adam can recognize his lack of direct kinship with animals. He needs another human. Eve mirrors him, differently. There is sameness, and there is otherness.

Cain perceives the otherness of Abel more acutely, and Cain's sharpened perception results in competitiveness and murder. Yet Cain goes on, with a sense of himself pitted against others and against the world, to found culture. He becomes the ancestor of those who create music and those who forge implements of copper and iron. There is an important connection between the awareness of otherness and the origin of culture. When we sense ourselves to be other than our surroundings, we create a world in which we can feel at home.

But radical otherness cannot serve as the basis for human life in this world; we must arrive at a fuller understanding of self. One approximation at such understanding is found in the story of Adam and Eve, a second in the story of Cain and Abel, and a third in the story of the Tower of Babel (Gen. 11:1–9). "All the earth had the same language and the same words" implies a negation of otherness. The single tongue is not the rich language developed by incorporating many different perspectives; it is comprised of the few words that remain when difference is suppressed.

A further response to otherness starts with God's call to Abraham, "Go forth from your native land and your kindred and your father's house to the land that I will show you" (Gen. 12:1). This call to radically reenvision the world marks the beginning of biblical instruction in the nature of the self.

While the call insists on obedience, it has no single meaning, just as there is no single response to the question "Who am I?" The call initiates a process that is repeated both throughout the Bible and within our own lives. "Go forth from your native land and your kindred and your father's house": we have all been called to find an understanding of self that transcends nationalism, tribalism, the authority of our historical roots, or our currently preferred pseudo-identity. We have all been called on a personal quest, although some of us may have rejected the call and accepted answers ready-made by our family, nation, or religious institution. The deepest quest we can undertake is the search for our identity and its role in the world. At the same time, we must remember that the search is both our quest and God's revelation: Abraham's quest started with God's call.

In Eden we needed no such quest, but leaving the Garden caused us to change from a state of naive unity to one of more complicated multiplicity. In Eden unity is assumed; there is no awareness of the differences and the unique qualities displayed by the other parts of creation. But differences do not rule out unity. We can recognize distinctions and still be led back to unity and the interconnectedness that underlies all diversity.

We have seen how the Hebrew scriptures offer five ways of rediscovering unity. Applying these methods to the story of Cain provides us with some insight into this troubling episode. Because the biblical account describing Cain's murder of Abel and his subsequent life is so brief, numerous folktales have risen up around the actual text that try to account for the gaps in the story. Cain's motivation for murdering Abel is unclear; God's choice of Abel's sacrifice over Cain's is not explained; and the concern God shows for Cain by bestowing on him a protective mark is puzzling. It is as if someone remembered a fragment of an important earlier tradition but something central was lost. The Bible makes clear that Abel dies without heirs. Cain marries and his offspring become the ancestors of those who found culture. Cain himself founds a city. Five generations later, the descendents of Cain give rise to the ancestor of all who dwell in tents amid herds and to the ancestor of all musicians. The same generation yields the forger of copper and iron implements. The relationship between Cain and culture is troubling. On the one hand, the Hebrew scriptures cast suspicion on many of the contributions that emanate from the line of Cain: cities are suspect, and metal instruments of war are not trusted (military faith should be placed in God, who would deliver the warriors). On the other hand, Abraham, the ancestor of all Jews, dwelt in tents amid herds, and King David, the most beloved of all the Hebrew Children, was the sweet singer of Israel who played the harp.

Cain, after killing his brother Abel, is sentenced to become "a ceaseless wanderer on earth" (Gen. 4:12). When the world is no longer home to us, we try to create a world in which we can feel at home. Cain's sentence motivates him to create culture. If the world at large becomes unfriendly to him, he creates a world in which he can thrive. Some people have tried to live their lives without resorting to any contribution from the line of Cain: they eschew advanced technology, avoid cities, and attempt to return to a simplicity they associate with the line of Abel or with his replacement, Seth. They try to see all good in Abel and all evil in Cain. But the Hebrew scriptures bring us back to unity by collapsing dualisms. If we refuse to inhabit cities, we must either become herders of livestock or tillers of the soil. The former occupation comes from the line of Cain, "the ancestor of those who dwell in tents and amidst herds" (Gen. 4:20), the latter from Cain himself, "and Cain became a tiller of the soil" (Gen. 4:2). We want to avoid Cain's flaw but not necessarily his gift.

Genesis does not record Cain's death, but follows instead the line of Seth, marking its births and deaths. Perhaps Cain's death passes without remark because he is deathless. While the scriptures trace all human life back to Noah, who comes from the line of Seth, we are today enveloped and created by the culture of Cain. Ernesto Galarza has written:

> I only sang
> because the lonely road was long;
> and now the road and I are gone
> but not the song.
> I only spoke
> the verse to pay for borrowed time;
> and now the clock and I are broken
> but not the rhyme.
> Possibly,
> the self not being fundamental,
> eternity breathes only on the incidental.[2]

Cain the person was not fundamental, but the cities, the herds, the music, and the forging of metal remain. The self should not be focused on but used. Cain, the biblical character, uses it to create the culture that makes up the world as we, its human inhabitants, now know it.

A binary way of thinking would lead us to assume that if Abel was good, Cain must have been evil. But the Hebrew scriptures refuse to cut off for all time any aspect of reality. Not only is Cain not cut off, he is protected, and his contributions lead to the cities of shame, Sodom and Gomorrah, on the one hand, and the city of refuge and peace, Jerusalem, on the other.

The tension in the text arises with Cain's punishment.

> Cain said to the Lord, "My punishment is too great to bear! Since You have banished me this day from the soil, and I must avoid Your presence and become a restless wanderer on earth—anyone who meets me may kill me!" The Lord said to him, "I promise, if anyone kills Cain, sevenfold vengeance shall be taken on him." And the Lord put a mark on Cain, lest anyone who met him should kill him. Cain left the presence of the Lord and settled in the land of Nod, east of Eden. (Gen. 4:13–16)

Cain wants to be in God's presence, an unusual desire for an "evil" person. He is presumably banished from God's presence, although God ensures that no one will kill him. Cain marries and fathers Enoch. Throughout the Hebrew scriptures, fertility is regarded as a gift of God, resulting not simply from insemination but from God's opening the womb. The long fruitful line of Cain belies banishment from God's presence. We might feel banished from the presence of God if we believe that God would fail to take notice, know, care, or remember. The presence of God is always associated with a sense of being noticed, remembered, and cared for: "I have marked well the plight of My people in Egypt and have heeded their outcry because of their taskmasters; yes, I am mindful of their sufferings" (Exod. 3:7). Cain's banishment is truly a nonbanishment: the detailed record of his line covers a full six generations.

Cain may, in one person, have lived many lives, but until Jacob no biblical biography shows a character whose development is brought about by life's experiences. We can only guess what major transformations might have been wrought in Cain's life. He is the first offspring. "Now the man knew his wife Eve, and she conceived and bore Cain, saying, 'I have gained a male child with the help of the Lord'" (Gen. 4:1). From being the only child in the world he goes on to become a sibling. While the meaning of Cain's name appears in the Bible (the name means "acquired," or "gained," as in "I have gained a male child"), the derivation of Abel's name does not. Cain is the actor in this drama, Abel merely the victim. Cain, after slaying Abel, goes on to become a parent, although the sibling rivalry is not repeated because he has only one son. But we can imagine that in the role of parent, he understands for the first time that Abel might have held value for his parents, and we can speculate that Cain could thereby have sensed his own responsibility. Because the story then switches from Cain to his descendants, we do not see how the tempering of time worked on Cain's character.

When we view the Bible as giving expression to aspects of the self, then we must claim Cain as part of the self and see that if we are Cain, we are also Abel. And the self, our self, that contains Cain and Abel also contains Adam and Eve. We learn that we are always confronting otherness—the otherness that is creative and fruitful and the otherness that is destructive and deadly. Otherness is not reducible to sameness, it is built into the very days of Creation, but underlying otherness is the one Source of all being.

Eve said, "I have gained a male child with the help of the Lord" (Gen. 4:1). Cain is a creation of God no less than Abel. And we remember once again the line from Isaiah, "I form the light, and create darkness, I make peace, and create evil" (Isa. 45:7).

2 | *Song*

In our examination of Creation, we were reminded that our deepest core is mystery. That is important to remember as we struggle to retain a sense of dignity when our socially constructed identity is challenged. But we need structures to help us explore the context within which we move to a radical reshaping of identity. The Bible formulates such a transformation in depicting the Israelites' change in status from a group of slaves to a nation of prophets and priests. Thinking about the Israelites in their enslaved condition forces us to consider just what belongs to us when we belong to someone else. We are forced to adopt a radical simplicity and made to think carefully what we could carry with us into the desert. The deprivations of slavery force us back into our own bodies: the beating of our hearts, the bowing of our heads, the rhythm with which we trudge along our path, these belong to us. We breathe, we lift, we turn, we bend—the rhythms of our labor are ours, and from these rhythms, from our bodies, our song arises. It is, indeed, our song that we carry with us as we move from slavery into freedom.

The Bible suggests that our consciousness is ordered musically and, specifically, that it is ordered and shaped by song. This view differentiates the consciousness of biblical thinking from that of Greek philosophy. The world comes to us through our senses: hearing, sight, taste, smell, touch, and awareness of body posture. When we try to assimilate all these sensations we tend to give priority to one mode of sensing over another in order to organize and report all of the sensory world.[1] The two dominant modes of sensing are sound and sight. In the Greek world, and hence for much of Western thought, sight had priority. In the biblical world, priority was given to sound. That distinction affects the positions we take on time, on transcendence, and on ethical imperatives.

The most significant meeting between God and the children of Israel took place at Sinai. At that quintessential moment, according to the theologian Samuel Terrien, God "was not seen—in any shape or in any mode. The auditive elements dominate: the thunders and the sound of the *shophar*. . . . A total darkness which is the symbol both of divine presence and of divine hiddenness . . . was a symbol of divine power in both its danger and its blessing."[2]

The Hebrew scriptures emphasize the primacy of sound over sight. This primacy is seen in the revelation at Sinai; in fact, whenever sight and sound are both mentioned, priority is given to sound:

> Take heed, you most brutish people;
>   fools, when will you get wisdom?
> Shall He who implants the ear not hear,
>   He who forms the eye not see?
>   (Ps. 94:8–9)

We can trace, in the Hebrew scriptures, the struggle for the dominance of one sense over the other. The dispute took the form of an argument between giving priority to "the name" of God, that is, the auditory aspect favored by the prophetic tradition, and giving priority to "the glory" of God, the visual aspect favored by the priestly tradition. Terrien concludes that

> the theology of the name affirms the sense of hearing at the expense of the sense of seeing. When the inquiring mind confronted the problem of revelation, the Deuteronomists offered him a cultic *anamnesis* which brought into the liturgical present the historical moment of the national birth. They said that God discloses his will for man but remains inaccessible to his sight. In so far as the human faculty of cognitive reason was associated with the sense of sight, the theologians of the name affirmed that God stands close to, but not within the grasp of man. . . . According to the theology of the name, man receives sufficient knowledge of God when he hears the word which he is bidden to obey in his daily life.[3]

Focusing on "the glory," with its stress on the visual and the spatially locatable, means emphasizing the sacred place, that is, the Temple and the hierarchy of people ministering there. Focusing on "the name" means emphasizing "the word" as moral imperative and deemphasizing ritual and the sacred place. Giving priority to sound and the word was not meant to exclude sight and the vision—God who implanted the ear also formed the eye—although the biblical struggle led both sides to take extreme positions. Millennia later, we can examine the hard-won view that sound should take priority without devaluing sight.

We may prize sound because our hearing develops before our sight. Even in the womb we hear the steady beating of our mother's heart. Sound becomes deeply ingrained months before our eyes first see light. But the priority of sound may have another source. When we see, the viewed object becomes part of our subjective sight, but when we hear, the sound displaces our sense of self. To truly hear another, we must get our self out of the way. A scripture whose major objective is a reformed notion of the self will move us toward such a change by emphasizing the sense of hearing.

The priority of sound over sight changes the stance of the religious person: "the mystic or philosopher 'sees and enjoys'; the man of the Bible 'hears and obeys.' "[4] In this statement, the theologian Will Herberg is really distinguishing between all those religious people whose primary sense is sight and all those whose primary sense is hearing. The biblical thinker finds intimacy with God in a moral imperative, not a beatific vision. When sound takes priority, salvation is not undertaken individually to achieve personal bliss, it is pursued by those who can hear, for the sake of all others.

Western thought depicts enlightenment as coming from darkness to light, a view based on the Greek primacy of sight. Plato's Allegory of the Cave regards most of the things people value as being mere shadows, or illusions, on the walls of a cave. In order to brings us closer to truth, Plato would have us turn toward the light. Moving from darkness to light would not be a natural metaphor for a people raised on the Hebrew scriptures. The Bible emphasizes an oral rather than a visual tradition. Where the Western philosopher fears darkness, the biblical thinker fears silence: "O God, do not be silent" (Ps. 83:2). Our own silence is not fearsome—it is essential, so that the voice of God can be heard, although God's silence is usually equated with aloofness.

The Bible speaks of the four hundred years of slavery in Egypt as a period of God's silence. While "the silence" became a sacred designation, someone had to remember that it stood in contrast to something else. Someone had to be ready after four hundred years to formulate the phrase, "the silence is over." Where God is silent there is no human history, and generations of silent beings blend into one another. In the time before the silence, every deed was fraught with meaning and, as we shall see, promises were amassed in sufficient number to make sense of all the remainder of human history.

The silence in Egypt had come gradually and in progressive stages. If we look back, we realize that it was built into the design of the world. Earlier stories tell of God speaking directly, thundering from the large expanse of sky. Even Abraham, however, had a touch of silence, or at least indirection: it was not God but an angel who stayed his hand on Mount Moriah. At that earth-shattering moment, at that confounding of all reason and triumph of paradox, should not God have spoken?

Isaac was "the silent." The silence was not only his toward God but God's toward him. God spoke *in* Isaac rather than *to* him, and used Isaac to play out tunes others might hear. We could say that God spoke *next to* Jacob. God's meetings with Jacob took place in dreams. These strange encounters at night comprised the extent of Jacob's communion with God. Joseph had no direct experience of God. He knew God only by inference, from his experiences and from his own insights into those experiences.

Perhaps the silence falls more swiftly when distinctiveness is lost. Perhaps it comes because the God of Abraham spoke to the oppressed and the oppressed have short memories. They have no art to embellish the stories, to sing them out, to unite them into one great saga. But the silence did come, for four hundred years of oppression in Egypt. Part of what it means to have been in slavery in Egypt is to have lived in a period of silence. If freedom is the ability to envision new possibilities, then living in a world that no longer speaks to us is being in bondage.

The people of the Bible differ from the prisoners in Plato's cave. The biblical characters, like Plato's prisoners, have firelight, but it comes from being seated around the campfire. If we take Plato's allegory literally and apply it to the biblical people, we find that what they see may be incomplete but it is not insubstantial. Their light comes from the glowing embers and the stars. But if they are to know one another, they must not get lost in the stars but remain focused on the shadowed presences around them who give the warmth that sustains them. Biblical people feel that they are where they are supposed to be. They are not estranged from a world of illusion but set down in a world designed for human habitation. They may need help, as Plato's prisoners did, but they do not need to be elsewhere.

Imagine this campfire at night, and imagine that out of the darkness a voice begins to sing with depth and resonance. Even though it is dark, the people around the campfire can still hear one another. The voice stirs something within them. Who were the narrators, the people who sang out their stories and imagined roles and meaning? They were those who experienced the surrounding world as unfamiliar and in need of explanation. Perhaps, as did Homer, they became narrators because the sensory world was different for them so they perceived it more vividly. Perhaps, like Aesop, they were unchosen so they imagined a drama that placed them more centrally. Let us imagine ourselves hearing the narrative. It is late at night and we shudder as a wind blows through the campsite. We wrap our dark robes tighter and close our eyes as the sonorous voice of the storyteller reaches us on a level deeper than the sense of the words. We might begin to doze and suddenly force ourselves awake. We watch the glowing embers in the campfire, then waken in a tent and do not remember how we got there or who had thrown a blanket over us. And as we trudge all day beside our families with the sonorous voice of the storyteller lingering in our muscles, we understand the story. It cannot be carried in papyrus sheets or in parchment scrolls, it must be carried in bones, joints, and flesh.

Stephen Crites makes a persuasive case for the inherent narrative quality of experience.[5] There are, he suggests, two types of stories: sacred stories that form our consciousness (rather than being objects of our consciousness) and mundane stories that help us clarify our sense of the world. In the biblical oral tradition, this argument is persuasive. Crites also suggests that action through time has an inherently musical style. Perhaps, then, the prior category is not narrative but song. The earliest narratives are thought to have been sung, and the song is even thought to have preceded its words. Similarly, the musical quality of experience has priority over the narrative quality. Melody, according to Mortimer Cass, originated in the sounds produced by the vocal apparatus of the earliest humans, sounds that expressed affect and reacted to external stimuli. Cass suggests that melody originally functioned to express emotion and that the melodic form probably antedated verbalization.[6]

Metaphysicians like to enumerate the minimum components

of reality: space, time, quality, relation. When Crites argues for the narrative quality of experience, he does not dispute the metaphysicians as much as he places their abstract arguments in a form we have all experienced. Arguing for the *musical* quality of experience does not dispute the narrative quality but emphasizes a different component. Inherent in music is time, understood as rhythm; structure, understood as the shape of the melodic line; and content, which is the actual thematic material of the melody. Added to these components is the quality of beauty, which is not something we hear, it is the way we structure and value what we hear. In entering the domain of music, we enter the realm of aesthetic judgment. Unlike the verbal use of vocalization, music is not primarily concerned with denoting. Its purpose lies in expressing emotional affect, and as such, judgments about music reside more in the domain of the beautiful than in the realm of truth.

Why should the world come to us musically? The world stands independent of our perception of it. Of this world, "the thing in itself," Kant says we have no knowledge, that we know only the world as it appears to us. As we attempt to think about this world as it appears to us, we find that it consists of time, space, and some principle of organization. To argue for the musical quality of experience is to say that the principle of organization is music, which consists not only of time (rhythm), and space (the shape of the melodic line), but also beauty (the evaluation of our perception). Kierkegaard disparages the organizing principle of beauty, relegating the aesthetic to the lowest level of his triumvirate of values. But Plato and many latter-day Platonists suggest that the beautiful, when fully analyzed, is identical to the good and the true. Beauty suggests that there is some principle of order, understanding, and fittingness that we need to get "hooked into" the world. Beauty is not a static concept—it depends on our correct perception. That is why God's revelation is a gift of beauty. At last we can grasp how things fit together and can affirm that "the heavens declare the glory of God" (Ps. 19:2).

The organizing principle of beauty may reveal a moral principle. This moral principle, while not a religious one (if religion is narrowly conceived of as a cultic practice), does foster the religious requisites of wonder and awe. Beauty is a principle of delight that enhances love and commitment. If beauty were an end in itself and were not rooted in some deeper mystery, it might be inadequate as an organizing principle. But according to Robert Grudin, beauty is

> the natural and necessary consequence of the proper interaction between subject and object.... Beautiful things are not only suitable to themselves but also display fitness for the greater hierarchies that they inhabit.... If beauty results from our insight into the integrity or fitness of phenomena, what are the effects of such insight? We may describe two sorts of effect: pleasure and love. Pleasure is the passive effect of beauty, the receptive sensation that, at the moment of insight or recognition, expresses itself, complete with adrenal burst, in wonder or laughter or tears. Love, on the other hand, is the active effect of beauty: the will to repeat or increase pleasure by participating in beauty as fully as possible.[7]

So a world whose organizing principle is beauty is one that we will enjoy deeply and participate in fully.

If we are to take seriously the *musical* quality of experience, we must examine the components of music: rhythm, melody, form, and words. Beat is part of what we mean by rhythm, just as pitch is part of what we mean by melody. We return to the womb, to the *ur*-song that accompanied our formation. The first component was beat. Beat is really only one process, whether we refer to respiration (inhaling and exhaling), creativity (building up and tearing down), or the life cycle (aging and becoming new). There is a rhythm to this, a natural beat that we can rage against or cooperate with. The beat accompanies our whole life: inhale, exhale; contract, release; defend, trust. We can drown out the natural beat in the prime of our life by building, contracting, grasping—but the beat continues incessantly, and at last we are ready to tear down, release, let go. If our awareness of the beat is not coerced, if it results from insight, we can recognize that exhalation is not diminishment but rather a new expansion, a new discovery of self. "A season is set for everything, a time for every experience under heaven.... A time for tearing down and a time for building up" (Eccles. 3:1–3).

The Bible treats time seriously. Time is understood in its several components:

> *Common time:* time marked to fix the festivals and sabbaths that allow for a shared understanding of the festive occasions. Common time is marked by something external to us, such as the phases of the moon. All too rarely do the festivals coincide with our feelings of joy, but the new moon arrives and so together, with the help of other people's convictions, we approach festival time.

Revelatory time: time as a medium of revelation. Our lives unfold developmentally and as we look back, we can discern how "God meant it for good." The only way to view an unfolding life is over time. Time makes a difference—we are affected by the trials, losses, achievements, and experiences we live through.

Sacred time: time as the locus for our meeting with God. Just as in the choice between sight and sound, the Hebrew scriptures opt for the less tangible and more intimate sense of sound, so in the choice between time and space, biblical thinking chooses time as the intangible but recurring and ever-available locus for sacred presence.

Given the priority of sound over sight, that of time over space logically follows. Space viewed from a sufficiently great distance can be seen at once, but no distance can allow one to hear all of sound at once. Sound, the song of life, unfolds over time. No matter how long and longingly we stare at a painting, we cannot finally merge with it, and it remains the object of our subjective consciousness. But music can allow for that union:

> ... music heard so deeply
> That it is not heard at all, but you are the music
> While the music lasts.[8]

One can be a serious, observant Jew and never visit the Holy Land, but one cannot be an observant Jew and never enter into the holy times of sabbath and the festivals. Entering into holy time effects a transformation of consciousness. Suddenly we are not the makers and doers of the workday, we are the grateful recipients of a world that sustains us prior to our acting upon it. And once again we are called upon to change our song:

> A psalm. A song; for the sabbath day.
> It is good to praise the Lord,
>   to sing hymns to Your name O Most High.
>   (Ps. 92:1-2)

While time is prior to space in biblical evaluation, it is not seen as a god or as an independent creation of God, but as a category dependent on our consciousness. The Hebrew scriptures instruct us not to regard time and space as illusory, but also not to regard them as ultimate. From God's perspective, we are told, "a thousand years/are like yesterday that has passed,/like a watch of the night" (Ps. 90:4). We cannot assume God's perspective, but realizing there is that perspective tempers the authority of our own. Also, knowing that our perspective *is* a perspective helps us gain some distance.

The notion that our consciousness is organized musically gains much support in the writings of Oliver Sacks. In treating patients suffering from "reminiscence," Sacks encountered two who heard inner music so loud that they confused it with outer music, thinking they were hearing a radio broadcast. One felt deeply gifted by the results of this music, while the other felt great distress. Sacks writes, "Both alike testify to the essentially 'melodic' . . . nature of inner life." He quotes with approval an aphorism by the German writer Novalis, "Every disease is a musical problem; every cure is a musical solution." In examining patients with severe motor disorders that cause tics, Sacks concluded that "ticcing 'unmusics'— as does Parkinsonism—and both *require* music, a single integrating motor and personal melody, to restore a true musicality (and personality) of movement and action."[9] His most powerful example of how music integrates and moves us appears in a study of his own leg surgery. After an accident and subsequent surgery, Sacks had become estranged from his injured leg. He no longer felt that the leg was his own or that he would know how to move it again.

> Suddenly, wonderfully, I was moved by the music. The music seemed passionately, wonderfully, quiveringly alive—and conveyed to me a sweet feeling of life. I felt, with the first bars of the music, a hope and an intimation that life would return to my leg— that *it* would be stirred, and stir, with original movement, and recollect or recreate its forgotten motor melody. I felt—how inadequate words are for feelings of this sort!—I felt, in those first heavenly bars of music, as if the animating and creative principle of the whole world was revealed, that life itself was music, or consubstantial with music; that our living moving flesh, itself, was "solid" music— music made fleshy, substantial, corporeal. In some intense, passionate, almost mystical sense, I felt that music, indeed, might be the cure to my problems—or, at least, a key of an indispensable sort.[10]

The idea that music is the creative animating principle of the world lies behind the biblical text "when the morning stars sang together" (Job 38:7). The line comes from God's speech to Job out of the whirlwind. God asks where Job was when God set the foundations for the world and when the morning stars sang together. There, at the very beginning of Creation, was the song that gave it life. First comes the music. Later words are introduced, and that is what allows us to memorize sagas of extraordinary length—the melody carries the narrative. We celebrate with song, we lament, we praise, and song is the shape of our journey.

We must distinguish between two types of song. The first is the song we all sing together only because we are human (just as the morning stars sang together without reference to their differences). The other song is the *particular* song that organizes our world, which, as Kant reminds us, is not *the* world, but the world as it appears to us, a world in which we can practice our vocation.

When the Children of Israel went forth from Egypt, they left slavery to become a nation of prophets and priests. Much happened that enabled them to integrate the change into their lives and perspectives. Notably, the first occurrence was that Miriam and Moses sang them a *new* song, the Song at the Sea: "The Lord is my strength and song; He is become my salvation" (Exod. 15:2). At a moment of terror and triumph, a song comforted the people, moved them to unity, and moved them forward on their journey. "The Lord is my strength and song" is a powerful refrain to carry into the unmarked wilderness.

We have music running through our heads. Sometimes we understand where it came from and what it is trying to tell us. It may be a song appropriate to the season or to common time, or it may be a song that expresses our feelings as we face a certain task. Sometimes we deliberately force the music out of our heads by singing a new song. Sometimes a melody haunts us, or a particular rhythm, or a lyric. That we become conscious only occasionally of the music running through our heads underplays its importance. It is there far more often than it is absent, and it serves to organize our orientation to reality. We are musical beings, rhythmical beings, beings affected by language. The song insinuates itself into our consciousness and then goes deeper and deeper, organizing the rhythm of our breathing and even the beating of our heart.

We go on a journey. We cannot carry along the view that inspires us, the monuments that quiet our fears, the many objects that signify home. But we carry our song, the song of home. The Lord's song can indeed be sung in every land. We carry it with us and sing it within.

We can outgrow our song. The song that sustains us in childhood may not be able to encompass our new sense of self. The song that fills our heart as we leave our lover may grow tired and worn as we reengage with life. Or we may hear a song one day that creates a yearning for something we had never dreamed of. But perhaps we are fortunate enough to have a song that is not drawn from the immediate exigencies of our dailiness. Perhaps our song can give shape to our very life. If we have learned the song well, we have shaped our life to its rhythm. Gradually we grow to fill in all the exquisite melismas. We do not stop growing, but we need not discard the song. It is our song, the song of our people, the song through which we have come to know God. It constitutes our being and consciousness. And just because we have internalized it so deeply, we can, with love and joy, improvise. Now our spontaneity comes to the fore, and we can be playful because we delight and love. When we first learn the song, variation and improvisation are unthinkable. But when our whole consciousness has been structured in terms of the song, improvisation is analogous to pushing against our own muscles to test their strength. We are not engaged in rebellion but in loving exploration of our song's capaciousness.

Improvisation is a form of freedom. When the Children of Israel learned the Song at the Sea, they were learning Miriam's and Moses' song of freedom. Even when they had learned it well, they had not yet internalized it. But when they could "sing unto the Lord a new song," they had moved into a freedom they could previously not even imagine. Each step is unimaginable from the viewpoint of the step before it. Moses could lead the Children of Israel out of bondage only because he himself had not been in bondage. From his awareness of physical freedom he could inspire the Israelites and lead them. But if it had been solely up to Moses, physical freedom would have been the limit of their attainment. The freedom offered to the Israelites was far more radical and transformative than a simple freedom from bondage. For that reason, they needed the experience in the wilderness and the revelation at Sinai to lead them to a greater understanding of freedom. True freedom requires more than the removal of constraints and even the ability to define alternatives and choose between them. "The creative mind exceeds this liberty in being able to redefine itself and reality at large, generating whole new sets of alternatives."[11] In this way freedom is related to identity and to a view of reality. The freedom celebrated in Exodus is really the freedom of creativity. Exodus teaches us to experience freedom as the unconstrained—it is a primer on how to envision new possibilities. A people of slavery are turned into a nation of prophets and priests by the same method that turns the closed, constricted view held by the slave into the openness and spirit of the prophet. The method is one of improvisation and creativity—learning to sing a new song.

Freedom is related to creativity and to the tasks we perform that express our identity. "This is the eternal origin of art, that a human being confronts a form that wants to become a work through him."[12] That is what we are here to do—the work of bringing the form to an artistic expression.

Freedom is not formlessness. Whether in the realm of musical improvisation or the realm of our very lives, freedom always occurs within an aesthetic form or way of life. So while form and time are components of both bondage and freedom, neither determines the condition. When time becomes an expression of what we think is important, then our time is our own and we are free. When our time is spent in ways unrelated to our values, then we are in bondage. Service to Pharaoh was bondage because it had nothing to do with the Israelites' identity. Service to God was no less demanding, but because it was consonant with what the Israelites believe was important, it turned out to be the deepest freedom.

If, as in Galarza's poem, "the road and I are gone but not the song," then perhaps we should identify with the song. It is not that we possess a song but that we somehow are constituted by a song, more specifically a ballad. We are a present that is deepened and nurtured by its past and projects toward its future. Remove our past and our identity is at risk. Foreclose our future and our sense of self trembles. We are a trajectory, not a frozen section or a still photograph. We are like the fronds of a fern, whose structure is determined by the structure of the larger whole. Our song, too, is determined by the structure of the people's song. Through the song of the people, we inherit our basic sense of life's rhythm, our understanding of space—including whether or not space points to a transcendent—and our views of quality and relation. All the unquestioned structures of our consciousness reside in the song of our people. Our consciousness, our basic categories of the understanding, and our self are structured by the people's song. Then our own song unfolds, one of the infinite variations of the larger song. We look at the larger song and challenge its focus or dispute a detail, not because we reject the song but because it has become ours.

Our lives go on, not consciously a microcosm of the larger song, but from time to time we recognize that a situation in our life reflects the larger song. The song creates both a people and its individuals, and in the process it gathers up our separate lives and makes sense of them within the larger song. A story has character development, a musical piece has thematic development; both are tempered by time.

Songs are not merely passed on, they are changed through deliberate improvisation. But they may also be changed because we mis-hear. Five people receiving a message hear five different messages. The major obstacle to hearing is the ambient noise. Quietness is a prerequisite: "Be still and know that I am the Lord."

The biblical medium is sound. We acknowledge the primacy of sound by our openness to silence. In silence we begin to gather the layers of our self, the self that is a song. At first we know the self in its emergence and in its relationship to the larger story, but then we know it in its relationship to other selves. We become who we are when we can speak to others and can distinguish their story from our own. Then we know the self in its quiet reflection on itself and its growing awareness of what hinders it. And finally, our self once again faces all of creation and discovers a self that is deeper even than suffering.

3 | *Appearance*

In our search for the self, our most basic tool is the distinction between appearance and reality—things as they seem and things as they are. We draw this distinction because the self is more than our naive apprehension of it. The appearance is not necessarily false, only incomplete. We use our senses to understand our world, but the world is not wholly intelligible through these sense impressions alone. We must finally arrive at an explanatory system that can account for what comes to us through our senses— that is, appearance—and to do that we actually turn *away* from the sense world. No matter how often we watch the sun make its circuit across the sky during the day, the appearance will always be that it rises and sets. Keeping that sense impression in mind, we search for some other explanation to account for the sun's apparent movement. Finally we conclude that the earth rotates on its axis. This reality does not negate the appearance, but it does warn us not to settle on the most obvious explanations for phenomena. Our senses alone are not sufficient for us to arrive at an understanding of the world around us.

The world at the time of the Tower of Babel was secular, not unlike the world of our own time. Looking back to that time, we recognize that God dispersed the people at Babel. Those at the Tower, however, knew only that their own world view was inadequate for what they had experienced. The people at Babel saw no difference between appearance and reality. The scriptures begin to draw this distinction with God's calling of Abraham. For the first time, we see a clear division between the world as it seems to everyone else and the world as it seems to Abraham. Abraham could see the rocks and trees and feel the heat and cold, just as everyone around him could, but he did not believe that these sensations exhausted reality. They were real, but they were not ultimate. Behind and beyond everything that he gained through his senses he perceived God. We might object that God's call to Abraham was not merely a matter of Abraham's interpretation, but that God was perceptible and forceful. But that is simply to say that God was real in Abraham's world.

Joseph's world more nearly resembles our own, in that no one of his generation encountered God (although God continued to appear to his father, Jacob, in a vision). Rather, as a fitting prelude to the silence and slavery of the Egyptian years, God was silent. The reality of God was inferred by Joseph from his own gift in interpreting dreams: a gift implies a giver.

Exodus represents the clash of two world views. Moses tried to show Pharaoh that while appearance suggested no power behind the impotent slaves, in reality God loved and cared for God's covenanted people. The plagues were an attempt to move Pharaoh from appearance to reality. But how many events can be interpreted in different ways? We call one thing coincidence, another bad luck. At what point does our interpretation become the finger or the hand of God?

At Sinai the Children of Israel shared Moses' world view. But in the day-to-day life in the wilderness they were drawn less to deeper explanations and more to the exigencies of daily life. Again we are reminded of our own quickening life with commitment that gets worn down in day-to-day living. But through the course of biblical history, the battle is always waged between those who accept appearance and those who push on to deeper levels.

As it was with the Children of Israel, so it is with ourselves and our own self-understanding. Do we accept ourselves as comprising only appearance, relationships, and actions, or do we, too, search for a depth dimension? Sigmund Freud suggests that "we are lived by unknown forces," as biblical a formulation as one can find. The statement in Genesis that we are created in the image of God precludes a reductionistic understanding of the self. Ultimately we recognize "unknown forces" that are the mystery lying at the heart of human identity. Freud's identification of manifest and latent content is very much in keeping with our distinction between appearance and reality.

Accepting this distinction entails our recognizing that the invisible gives rise to the visible. The visible, or sensible, cannot finally explain itself. The Psalmist grapples with this notion:

> I saw a wicked man, powerful,
>> well-rooted like a robust native tree.
> Suddenly he vanished and was gone;
>> I sought him but he was not to be found.
>> (Ps. 37:35–36)

The appearance is that the man is "well rooted," the reality is still on the level of appearance, but "suddenly he vanished and was gone." But the Children of Israel were groping for a depth dimension, a deeper reality, than the world of appearance. The Bible consistently emphasizes this difference between appearance and reality, and teaches us to look for the deeper reality. The tattered beggar may be a secret saint. Behind the distinction between appearance and reality lies the realization that each person, despite a degraded appearance, is created in the image of God.

The same distinction is exemplified by Joseph's statement to his brothers, who had sold him into slavery: "You meant evil against me, but God meant it for good." What had appeared to Joseph to be evil—being sold into slavery—was in reality good, because he was placed in a position where he could preserve life. Joseph's capacity to recognize the real good in the apparent evil is one we must try to develop. We must learn, as he did, to discern chosenness in the face of our oppression.

The distinction between appearance and reality is a variation of the historical tension in Judaism between sight and sound that is spelled out in the conflict between the priestly and prophetic traditions. The priests focused on the glory, which was visible, and tried to locate it spatially in the Temple in Jerusalem. The emphasis on sight gave rise to an institutionalized cult with a hierarchical authority. The prophets, on the contrary, focused on the word and located it in the still, small voice within us all. This emphasis retained the idea of a *nation* of priests and prophets, as opposed to a hierarchy. As noted earlier, sound is both temporally prior to and physically closer than sight. It is also more intimate than sight: in order to see we must look without, but in order to hear we must attend to the sound within.

Abraham *perceived* rather than *sensed* the presence of God. Every perception is an act of constructing and construing the world. When we sense, we passively take in sense data; when we perceive, we actively interpret our sensations. It would be wonderful if Abraham's awareness of the distinction between appearance and reality were passed down flawlessly from generation to generation. But we do not awaken to that distinction once and never fall asleep to it again. In reading Ecclesiastes we are reminded that even after accepting the reality of God, we may be unable to *perceive* God's effectiveness in our lives. That which is real has real effects. To say that God is real and to deny any consequences to God's reality is altogether self-contradictory. Ecclesiastes gets around the contradiction by saying that God *had* effect in creating the world and God *will have* effect in the judgment after death, but in the present God has no effect that would allow us to experience life as meaningful. The Book of Ecclesiastes is not simply the nihilistic view of a disillusioned individual, it is a text that speaks to each of our lives. There comes a time when we may experience that weariness. While we are always called to transcend appearances, our overwhelming perception of apparent injustice and meaninglessness may make us lose heart, as the Israelites did.

People frequently wonder at the Israelites' inability to feel close to God after witnessing a miracle, the parting of the Red Sea. Shouldn't a miracle once and for all convince us of reality's depth dimension? But a miracle is not an event, it is the interpretation of an event. How much has already occurred in our lives that could be interpreted as miraculous but that we stubbornly dismiss as—coincidence? chance? good luck? Even when we are prepared to call an event a "miracle," are we prepared to *remember* its miraculous qualities for years?

An acquaintance related the following:

> After the birth of my first daughter I lay in awe and bliss, thinking that I must be feeling the way that God felt after Creation. It was good; it was very good. I could not get over the wonder of this life, so little and so complete. There had been nothing, and now there was—a person! The years passed, and the child became an adolescent. Blessedly, I *did* remember. Even as I asked her to clean her room, another part of my mind was saying, "her being is a miracle."

The dual vision is not dualism and does not thrust us out of Eden; it is what allows us to perceive the depth dimension. The room is dirty *and* the room's owner is a miracle.

This dual vision exemplifies the biblical way of construing the relationship of appearance to reality. In that view, appearance participates in reality. The biblical view impels us to reengage with this world. In the Platonic world view, appearance mimics reality, that is, this ephemeral world imitates an enduring, changeless model. Our allegiance is to the changeless world of forms, not to this all-too-transitory material world, which is deemed to be a distraction. Our goal is to transcend this world in our quest for reality, a goal that some Western religious thought adopted from the Greek philosophic tradition.

The message in Plato's Allegory of the Cave differs significantly from the biblical one. Plato is attempting to change our basic belief, that we are looking at reality clearly and seeing it as it is. He is saying that, on the contrary, we are not seeing reality at all, only shadows on the walls of a cave. Not only do we not see reality, we do not even see ourselves. Altogether, our perception is not what it should be. Taking Plato's metaphor seriously requires us to undergo a conversion experience. We must turn away from the shadows on the wall of the cave—the material world—in order to perceive reality. The Bible, on the other hand, asks us not to turn away from the world but to enter into it ever more deeply. We are told that the world is not fallacious or misleading, it is just not complete. The world does not explain itself nor does it exhaust itself, and we cannot understand it on its own terms. The world points beyond itself to its source. The Bible demonstrates that the sacred is not distinct from the ordinary, although we cannot as yet see that. Turning away from the world can be a way into silence (and we will explore those benefits in chapter 5), but finally we must return to the world, because only in its depths can we begin to sense the reality that underlies and supports it at every point.

The difference between the Platonic and the biblical views of reality and appearance determines our relationship both to the material world and to recent scientific discoveries. Scientists might dismiss the view that there is a reality deeper than their own conceptual system, a reality that underlies and supports their system. Platonists might dismiss the material world as not worthy of engagement. But persons holding the biblical view must integrate scientific discoveries without believing that they explain anything exhaustively and must embrace the material world as revealing of reality. William Blake took on the scientists of his time in his call for the double vision:

Mock on, mock on, Voltaire, Rousseau;
Mock on, mock on; 'tis all in vain;
You throw the sand against the wind,
And the wind blows it back again.

And every sand becomes a gem,
Reflected in the beams divine;
Blown back, they blind the mocking eye,
But still in Israel's paths they shine.

The atoms of Democritus
And Newton's Particles of light
Are sands upon the Red Sea shore
Where Israel's tents do shine so bright.[1]

Many scientists share the view that lies behind the calling of Abraham—the view that the world is more than merely what we see—and that we must attend to the force behind and through the world. But their understanding of "the force" is often reduced to a physical law formulated perhaps in terms of gravity or of magnetism. The biblical and scientific views agree that a distinction must be drawn between appearance and reality if we are to search for the deepest sense of the self, but the biblical view would push the scientists further and say that behind their material laws lies a deeper reality. The scientists are not wrong, they just present an incomplete picture.

Plato's distinction between appearance and reality also differs from the Bible's distinction in its appraisal of time. Plato values the timeless, and therefore unity and the changeless. According to this view, change (the world of becoming, or coming to be and passing away) is less real and less valuable than the changeless (the world of being). Change, in fact, is seen as a threat. Knowledge is limited to the changeless, so change renders whatever it touches unfit for knowledge and subject only to true belief.

The world of the Hebrew scriptures values change. Time is regarded not as an obstacle to knowledge but as the actual medium of revelation. Revelation came to the Children of Israel at a specific time in history. That their revelation continued is seen in God's ongoing relationship with them as depicted in the Bible. The Israelites' continuing relationship to God is transformative, and time is the medium through which this transformation takes place as they come to resemble more closely who they are meant to be.

For the Platonist an essential self persists through all the changes. For the biblical follower, the self is an ongoing creation shaped by the choices made and by the graciousness of God's interaction. The Bible shows how the experiences and choices we make create our character. Judah, who conspired with his brothers in Joseph's kidnapping, becomes dismayed by the role he played and so moves away from his other brothers to marry and raise a family. The loss of his first two sons tempers him. Then his widowed daughter-in-law, Tamar, uses a ruse to become pregnant by him. But when she accuses him of withholding his last son, who was to marry her under the terms of levirate marriage, he publicly declares that she is more righteous than he. It is only within the context of his life experiences that we can understand his transformation, which is further revealed in his moving speech pleading to the now-empowered Joseph on Benjamin's behalf. It was not that Judah had a noble character that was at last revealed, but that the experiences of his life following Joseph's kidnapping made him truly repentant. The biblical follower is concerned with particular choices not because they *reveal* character but because they *create* character. According to the biblical view, we are shaped by the decisions we make, time makes a difference, and change is real.[2] In comparing the Platonic and biblical traditions, we face the question: Is there some essential self that persists through these changes and that constitutes our real identity, or is the self to be created and we participate by the choices we make in creating our self?

The Hebrew scriptures also show the value and significance of time by offering many portraits of aging, which is itself a form of revelation. The first fully drawn portrait of aging in the Bible is that of Jacob. Later, we see Joseph move over time from pampered youth, to frightened enslaved adolescent, to powerful prime minister, to a person who has achieved an adult relationship with his brothers, and finally to a man with a deathbed vision of the Israelites' eventual exodus from Egypt.

From the biblical perspective time is real, and its changes are not merely accepted but welcomed as gifts. The Bible shows the arrogant youth tempered to become the humble sage. So we cannot draw the distinction between appearance and reality in the biblical world view in terms of the Greek world view's distinction between the timeless and the temporal.

Because biblical followers value change, they also value multiplicity. The world of change *is* a world of multiplicity, and in one lifetime we live many lives. We are the naive child full of enthusiasm but without direction, the unformed youth tentatively trying a path, the arrogant adult who has found not only a personal way but *the* way, and the compassionate elder who admits mistakes and has learned to forgive. We incorporate multiplicity within ourselves and we see and celebrate it all around us. Only in the unchanging world of Plato's forms can multiplicity be avoided.

Out of these many differences between the biblical and the Greek philosophical world views, a new perspective on history and personal history emerges. When time and change are real, we sense that we *can* make a difference. We can change the world, or at least contribute toward changing it. The biblical view of time and change directly influenced the prophetic tradition. If change is possible, then it is a moral imperative. "At the heart of the Jewish vision of history was the Jews' sense that they had a task they had not completed, a task that required time."[3] The basic task for the Children of Israel is *tikkun olam*, healing the world. "You are not called upon to complete the work, yet you are not free to evade it."[4] Where Plato focuses on the real world of the forms, the Children of Israel focus on *this* very real world to which they are passionately committed.

Another assumption underlies Plato's distinction between appearance and reality. Plato actually presents more than the two categories of real and apparent; he is committed to an entire scale of values from the unreal to the real. He believes that there are degrees of reality that directly parallel degrees of value, that is, what is most real is most valuable. Although Plato is usually portrayed as a simple dualist, his belief in the entire continuum from unreal to real suggests a more subtle formulation. We know that we are striving to become more authentic. We can hardly become so "unreal" as to disappear, but we find full authenticity to be equally elusive. Reality is something we can only approach. We seek to get beyond illusions but come up against belief systems, habits, and aspects of cultural conditioning that obstruct our perception of reality. The view that there are degrees of reality resembles the biblical view that the material world has genuine being and value but has less ultimacy and value than its source.

The call to Abraham demonstrates our need for a stimulus that forces us to reflect on the world in which we live. The world does not explain itself. Abraham's call to leave his homeland and his father's house suggests that we, too, cannot simply accept the stories we have heard from our parents, we must move beyond them and look ever more deeply for the real.

After the calling of Abraham, God ceases working through individual characters in the Bible to work through the family and, later, the people. As a people our individual strengths can be enlarged even as our separate weaknesses can be compensated for. Being alone gives us a sense of unreality. The self and its own sense of reality depends on the interrelationship of selves. We discover that we may seem to be searching individually but we carry within us the world views of our family and culture. We are not essentially alone, we are essentially in relationship. The self internalizes language and values, and constructs itself socially. We now undertake deliberately what happened to us in a haphazard way because of who our parents were, with whom we came in contact, and what stories played formative roles in our development.

In the Haggadah for Passover, we read that in every generation it is our duty to see ourselves as though we personally had come out of Egypt, according to the biblical injunction, "You shall tell your son on that day: This is because of what the Lord did for *me* when I came out of Egypt" (Exod. 13:8). "It was not only our ancestors whom God set free from slavery; along with them he freed us too, as it is written, 'He brought us out from there that he might bring us home, to give us the land which he had pledged to our ancestors.'"[5]

Not only are we not by ourselves, we are not for ourselves. We receive a clearer vision of reality, not for our enjoyment, but for the purpose of sharing it with others and utilizing it in our efforts on behalf of this world.

When God works through an entire people, the major obstacle is settlement. The Children of Israel must wander for forty years in the wilderness because settling is dangerous, since we are called to distinguish appearance from reality, and settlement represents our refusal to probe. Settlement is "settling" for appearance; it represents our becoming weary and refusing to travel further.

Settlement means repressing the knowledge that we are called to a deeper quest and accepting something less than reality. It means that we have distracted ourselves from our own longings. Distraction can take the form of accepting inadequate identities: we are our status, our possessions, our fame, even our habits and addictions. But to accept wandering is to heed the call to keep searching and to go beyond all appearances to the reality that grounds them.

4 | *Memory*

We have honed our fundamental tool, the distinction between appearance and reality, and now must begin our quest for the self. We do not apply this tool to the raw material of sight, sound, taste, smell, and touch, but rather to memory, a structure already built out of these raw materials.

Abraham was called to go beyond country, kindred, and his father's house. That is not to say that these facts of his existence were unimportant, just that they were not final. If we wish to arrive at what *is* final or more nearly foundational, we must deal with the given facts of our own existence. These facts come to us through our memory and that, as we have already noted, is not raw, unconsidered, and unstructured. Memory must be carefully entered into and reconstructed to empower us on our quest.

Much of the Bible is concerned with forming a shared memory and context in which to set individual lives. It is useful to examine this process of forming a shared memory because the quest for the self is the same for an individual as it is for a people.

Psalm 77 demonstrates one of the functions of memory. It begins in deep despair:

> I cry aloud to God;
> I cry to God that He may give ear to me.
> In my time of distress I turn to the Lord,
> with my hands uplifted;
> my eyes flow all night without respite;
> I will not be comforted.
>
> (Ps. 77:2–3)

But after the initial complaint the Psalmist puts the personal anguish within the context of the people:

I recall the deeds of the Lord;
  yes, I recall Your wonders of old;
I recount all Your works;
I speak of Your acts.

(77:12–13)

The trust of the Psalmist's forebears had been warranted:

You are the God who works wonders;
  You have manifested Your strength among the peoples.
By Your arm You redeemed Your people,
  the children of Jacob and Joseph.

(77:15–16)

According to this psalm, the history of the Israelites is still being written; revelation continues in the unfolding of the people's lives, and it will be a triumphant history. The theologian Kathleen Fischer points out that "at each key juncture in her life, Israel retold the story of what God had done for her, how God had remained faithful in the midst of her infidelities, how God's presence had sustained her in times of trial. By remembering she made God's love present again with power." In fact, she recalls, "as the philosopher Alfred North Whitehead tells us, memory is really another word for presence."[1]

We must also recount the history of the Children of Israel because we know that all children lack the memory of sorrow healed, so their grief is all-consuming. As we age, we experience losses and the healing of those losses, followed by a renewed commitment to life. Knowing that we have the ability to deal with pain empowers us to face new crises with hope.

Shared memory also helps us make sense of the present and enables the Children of Israel to call for God's help with some confidence that their shared history with God justifies the demand:

We have heard, O God,
  our fathers have told us
  the deeds You performed in their time,
  in days of old.

(Ps. 44:2)

In days of old God had given them a land and won battles for them, but now:

Yet you have rejected and disgraced us;
  You do not go with our armies.

(Ps. 44:10)

But this rejection is felt to be unjustified. The Children of Israel have been true to the covenant and have not sought out foreign gods. Because of their faithfulness, they feel justified in demanding God's faithfulness:

> Arise and help us,
> redeem us, as befits Your faithfulness.
> (Ps. 44:27)

The psalm ends with this plea, along with the sense that it is reasonable and the faith that it will be fulfilled.

Psalms 78 and 105 tell the basic story of the Israelites in two very different ways. Psalm 78 focuses on the people's unworthiness, inconstancy, and stubbornness. It justifies the installation of an absolute monarch who will shepherd this backsliding nation. Psalm 105 says nothing about the people's unworthiness but invokes the wonders that God performed for their sake when bringing them out of Egypt. The self shaped by the story in Psalm 78 needs control, rules, laws, priests, and monarchs. The self formed by Psalm 105 is destined to be in perpetual tension with the self modeled on Psalm 78.

Our memories, like those of the Israelites, can be told either in ways that assign blame and guilt or in ways that emphasize gratitude and wonder. Like the Children of Israel we all acknowledge that our story is part of a larger story. "Individual lives appear to have little meaning out of the context of history and family."[2] For a major part of our lives we may not be interested in that larger story, nor do we want our lives simply to reflect our parents' future. We feel continuity with our parents but not identity. In our quest for self we must confront their otherness. But the most haunting and challenging otherness we must face is an earlier form of ourselves.

Robert Grudin wrote of intelligent individuals that "their past is no more finished or dead than their ability to understand it."[3] The past remains an ever-fertile field for us to plow. We keep returning to it with new tools of understanding, new insights gleaned from our enlarged experience. How could we have understood our parents before we ourselves had parented? But as we find ourselves torn between a desire to give our children autonomy and an urgent need to protect them, we understand the strained tone in our own parents' voices a generation earlier.

"Only the present is fixed; the past is always changing."[4] We continually rewrite the past in light of our present understanding.

When we were children, the gift of a paintbox was lost amid the general festivities of a birthday celebration. But later, as we see our future moving toward a vocation as artist, receiving that childhood gift becomes a moment imbued with deep significance.

Memory can inspirit us when we must pass through trials. It can serve as a warrant for future hope and can validate our chosen identity. But memory is fraught with pitfalls. The Hebrew Scriptures demonstrate the dangerous aspect of memory as well. The story of Lot's wife tells us about memory and about freezing up when we look back. Lot's wife turns into a pillar of salt to symbolize her grief and tears when she cannot go beyond her past. "The way through the past involves the danger that some people never reach the goal because they get lost somewhere."[5] We do have to reclaim the past—the joyous as well as the painful—but we must do it in a way that will not paralyze us. Until we can take on the pain, we cannot take on the rest of our lives. We all know people who do not seem quite three-dimensional: those who cannot claim their past lose a dimension of self.

Not all loss of the past results from an inability to assimilate the pain. Sometimes, in aging, the memory cells are damaged. Is someone whose memory cells are destroyed still the same person? What is the relationship of memory to identity? An elderly victim of Alzheimer's disease is someone whose continuity has been broken, and if that is the person who held our experiences together, our own identity feels threatened. In infancy our self cannot hold its own experiences, so our parents hold them in trust until we can claim them. But we cannot hold the aged person's experiences. However close the resemblance between caring for the infirmed elderly and caring for an infant, there are important differences. Infants will grow into their experiences, but the elderly will not regain their memories. Infancy and Alzheimer's lead us onto two different paths: one to integration and effectiveness, the other to deeper and deeper dissociation, ending in death. Looking at people with Alzheimer's shows us how important a role memory plays in identity.

> You have to begin to lose your memory, if only in bits and pieces, to realize that memory is what makes our lives. Life without memory is no life at all.... Our memory is our coherence, our reason, our feeling, even our action. Without it, we are nothing.... (I can only wait for the final amnesia, the one that can erase an entire life, as it did my mother's.)[6]

Oliver Sacks uses this quotation by Luis Buñuel as an epigraph to his chapter dealing with a patient suffering from Korsakov's syndrome, a profound and permanent devastation of memory that can be brought on by the use of alcohol. Memory is an essential aspect of the self, but "a man does not consist of memory alone," according to the neurologist A. R. Luria. "He has feeling, will, sensibilities, moral being—matters of which neuropsychology cannot speak."[7] Sacks searches for something that can hold the attention of this patient and finds three areas in which the patient seems almost normal: attending mass, working in the garden, and perceiving a work of art. Structures—religious, natural, aesthetics—can for a short time replace the continuity normally provided by memory.

The British empiricist George Berkeley asserted that things exist only when they are being perceived. In order to account for the world's not flying off into nothingness, he postulated that God sees everything, so that even when we forget to perceive the world, it still exists. Analogously, the Children of Israel can speak of the God who remembers even the memories they forget; they can feel assured that nothing finally gets lost. The Israelites came out of Egypt after four hundred years of oppression with no memory of a larger context. Taken out of their oppressive but familiar routine, what would hold their identity in the wilderness? Sacks found that his patient with Korsakov's syndrome was "held" by a relationship to music and art. "[The patient] had no difficulty ... 'following' music or simple dramas, for every moment in music and art refers to, contains, other moments."[8]

A musical theme is introduced. It is developed. Tension is introduced, building toward a climax. We hear a resolution approach. Then, with simplicity and a powerful quietness, the original theme returns. The effectiveness of the theme's development results from our recalling the original theme and experiencing its embellishment and transformation, feeling the tension, and anticipating the climax. The resolution moves us because we are returned to the innocence of the theme's introduction. Just as the patient with Korsakov's syndrome could be held by music, the Children of Israel could also be held initially by the Song at the Sea.

The Song at the Sea is important both because it *is* a song and because it is a shared statement about reality, so those who sang it could gain a sense of community. Finally, it is important because it gave the Israelites the foundation of their future story and their basic historiographical principle: all is to be interpreted in terms of their relationship to God. Being aware of the dimensions of time holds special importance for Grudin:

> Those people who can, relatively speaking, control and inhabit their own past and future, have a particular dignity. . . . Self-respect is impossible without respect for one's own past, and. . . coherent action in the present is impossible unless it is based on a vision that extends with some specificity into the future.[9]

We, like the Children of Israel, must claim our enslaved condition, comfort the earlier form of our self, and move into the Promised Land. But the people of the Exodus were not the people who reached the Promised Land. The entire generation of adults at the Exodus found their own reward not in reaching the Promised Land but in identifying with their children who would reach it. There is a close relationship between claiming our past and being able to enter into the future, which entails, in part, loving and identifying with our children. Grudin describes the experience of loving children and feeling his own future expand and stretch with theirs as "transfiguring."[10]

It is difficult to imagine the terror that the Israelites experienced in the wilderness. They had broken from everything they had previously known, and with no past and no way to think about the future, they were thrust into a desert devoid of landmarks to aid them. Stanley Keleman writes, "The memory of our lives is the attempt to keep an unbroken stream of feelings, thoughts, and actions going. We want to believe our lives are totally continuous. . . . A moment of discontinuity is like loss, with all its emotional responses."[11] So part of the anguish the Israelites felt in the desert was inspired not only by their lack of food and water, but by their lack of social structures and identity. Keleman writes further,

> Most of us tend to project our social roles into the future in the hopes of keeping the future stable. It is these socialized roles that we fear losing because we equate them with existing. To lose our roles is to fear losing our continuity. Futurizing is part of living. The projection of ourselves into the future extends our existence and guarantees the continuity of our ongoingness.[12]

When the Children of Israel entered the wilderness they lost their past social roles and could not project into the future. But the time in the wilderness was spent in forging a new identity. Past help became a warrant for future hope. "People who plan ahead . . .

can escape despair. They have cast tow-lines out to the future and can, when necessary, drag themselves through a becalmed or stormy present."[13]

Israel Baal Shem Tov said that forgetfulness is exile, remembrance is redemption. Elie Wiesel brings home a similar point in relating the following parable:

> Wanting to punish his son, the king sends him into distant exile. Suffering from hunger and cold, the prince waits to be recalled. The years go by; he has lost the very strength to wait for the royal pardon. Then, one day, the king sends him an emissary with full powers to grant the prince's every desire and wish. His message delivered, the emissary waits for the prince's instructions. [The Prince] asks him for a piece of bread and a warm coat, nothing else. He has forgotten that he is prince and that he could return to his father's palace.[14]

If the Children of Israel could remember that God had been with them in Egypt and was with them now in the wilderness, then the wilderness would be redemption. Without that memory, the wilderness would be felt as an exile from the fleshpots of Egypt. The Israelites needed to remember not merely that they were delivered from Egypt, but that their redemption took place because of their relationship to God, which lay at the heart of their identity. The Children of Israel are, as we all are, children of God, and that memory would form their identity in the wilderness. How forgetfully and tragically we undername our lives. The Bible's task is to help us remember just who we are.

Perhaps the greatest benefit for the Israelites of their reconstructed memory was the way it prepared them to receive revelation. "Inspiration is profoundly linked to memory. ... To the inspired as well as to their audiences, innovative insights contain a sense of the familiar, the permanent. Inspiration may be the revelation of something completely new, but it is also the rediscovery of something always true."[15] The Israelites knew that what Moses reported to them was indeed revelation because they experienced a deep sense of familiarity and fittingness in what they were told.

> On the third day, as morning dawned, there was thunder, and lightning, and a dense cloud upon the mountain, and a very loud blast of the horn [shofar]; and all the people who were in the camp trembled. Moses led the people out of the camp toward God, and they took their places at the foot of the mountain.
> Now Mount Sinai was all in smoke, for the Lord had come

down upon it in fire; the smoke rose like the smoke of a kiln, and
the whole mountain trembled violently. The blare of the horn grew
louder and louder. (Exod. 19:16–20)

The *shofar* that grew louder and louder at Sinai serves as a
powerful symbol for Rosh Hashanah (New Year's Day), the "Day
of Remembrance." The sound comes from outside but touches
deep within. It is stirring, and we cannot "tame" it by assigning
one specific meaning to it. Significantly, the symbol for the Day of
Remembrance is a sound. While the first sounds we heard were
in utero, the reassuring sound of our mother's heartbeat, the shofar's sound is not restful. It is meant to awaken and arouse us
from forgetfulness.

The shofar announced the revelation at Sinai, but what was
revealed? The first irreducible content was presence: God had
been with them, God was with them, God would be with them.
Throughout the Hebrew Bible, the Children of Israel are admon-
ished to care for the stranger, for they had themselves been
strangers in a land not their own. Their enslavement could lead to
compassion rather than bitterness because God had witnessed all
that they had suffered ("God shall number all your tears"),
affirmed that they were valuable even while their oppressors were
telling them that they were worthless, and could see that their
suffering was unjust. God's presence transformed their slavery
from a value judgment about them to a trial they successfully sur-
vived, and it transformed the Israelites' sense of identity. God's
continuing presence is the key to their self-understanding, "for
what does it mean to be Israel except to be ready to separate, to
venture into an unknown land and time, with God alone as
steersmate, and with no identity save that of God's conscious
creature?"[16] All that happens to them, bad as well as good, takes
on significance only in terms of their relationship to God. And
God's promise to be with them is that projection into the future
which allows them to leap across the void held only, like the spi-
der, by a slim thread.

We have identified with the Children of Israel, using their
story as a way to express and understand our own transformation. As we face the uncertainties of our way, we cling to God's
promise to be with us.

5 | *Desert*

Our quest for a more authentic sense of self begins when the identity we arrive at proves to be provisional and, finally, inadequate. The quest is aided by an examination of memory. The journey of the Israelites continues to provide a structure through which we confront our fears and purge all that obstructs our coming into selfhood.

The time spent by the Israelites in the desert would forge their identity and deepen their understanding of freedom. But their entry into the desert was not without anguish. "[Israel] does not want to enter the wilderness that symbolizes the loneliness of its life with a God in whom other nations do not believe; ... the life it did not want to lead was the only life it could."[1] The Israelites' ambivalence about the desert is mirrored in our own experience. A French Saharan explorer once said that "the desert is probably the most intensely loved landscape on our earth,"[2] but that love is mixed with the anxiety and forlornness of the setting. The desert is certainly the ideal surrounding in which to grasp the meaning of freedom. All the Israelites' roles, customs, and habits in Egypt are lost in the boundless expanse of the desert. There are no signposts. The desert is a place of barren landscape and, even more, of silence—silence so absolute that we can hear and even feel the blood coursing through our body. Absolute isolation reigns, and memory is essential for survival, because no new story can be heard.

The Israelites' prime concern on entering the desert is whether they can survive there. They express their fear through doubts that they would get enough food and water to survive. The early chapters of Exodus deal extensively with water, food, and finally, the Israelites' desire for meat. What they see when they view the desert is absolute barrenness. It might seem as if the only life they could hope to find there is what they themselves had brought. But there is life in the desert, surprising life untrammeled by domestication: hidden springs of water and startling growth that is shaped by solitude, fierce temperature changes, and harsh winds.

A tree grows in the desert. It grows downward until it reaches a deep water vein with its roots, and only then does it grow outward. That tree represents an important message for the Children of Israel: they must turn deep within to find the source for nourishment and only then grow outward toward a settled place.

We imbue the desert with our hopes, anticipations, fears, and expectations, but then the awareness that most of our surroundings are of our own making frightens us. What is real, and what have we projected onto the barren landscape? Those experiencing the desert know sooner than city dwellers or tillers of the field the emptiness that only God can fill. If we stand in the desert and for a moment see no other form, no trace that any human had been there before, the desolation overwhelms us. We find the desert inhuman, but learn to live with it and so prepare ourselves for an encounter with God. Normally we see God in terms of our expectations. We get the God we imagine, not because God is imaginary but because we can be open only to what we can imagine. But when we are truly open, without expectations, we experience the great openness—nothingness, or desert. *Desert* is also a name for God.

We keep creating our world. We try to make our creation richer and deeper with meaning by tying it to time, memory, and tradition. But memory and tradition are also artifacts. We need one another to make this world real; we need the shared affirmation of meaning and value that allows us to create a functioning world. In the desert we are alone, facing the blank canvas of nature. We stop projecting, grow quiet, and wait to discover what was there before we created.

The desert fed an oral tradition, but not one that emphasizes "the word" as rational principle. The Children of Israel were a desert people, and there is no *logos* in the desert. Their oral tradition is that of the word sung around the campfire. As nomads, they travel light, carrying no icons. They pass through the desert, sometimes piling stones to leave a mark, but always rolling up their tents so that nothing remains of their noisy presence after they have broken camp. A wind blows away the remnants of grain, the grounds from their drink, and the ashes from their campfires. But they carry their stories with them—landmarks no wind can disperse.

The desert is, physically, the land lying past the borders of settlements, but metaphorically it is the uncharted and surprising that resides within and beneath the ordinary. Even so, it is not domesticated by the ordinary, and it can cause the ordinary to surprise us with its beauty and, sometimes, with its strangeness. Suppose one day you can't catch your breath because a chicken bone is caught in your throat. And then it is freed. You tell two, three, four people about your brush with death, and with each telling the close call becomes more distant. Finally it is just one more story to recount. That moment when we were poised on the brink of being is transformed by repeated telling. If we stare at our vulnerability too long, the whole world threatens to fly apart. What we have done is step into the domain of awe. The usual landmarks are gone, and even unusual ones are lacking. Only a long commitment to trust keeps us poised in this strange uncharted place, where the call is as clear as our awareness of how frightened we are of the call. Our ordinary environment—so comfortable, so settled—must be released. Beneath it and supporting it lies the reality that is deeper than appearance and that calls for our commitment. We return to the surface, to the familiar shape of things, but we have heard the call and part of our attention remains focused on the barren landscape. The surface has been irrevocably stirred.

Life and death are part of the desert's challenge; more important is the awareness we gain of the question of meaning. The desert forces us to assess what is real and what finally commands our allegiance. In the tradition of the Hebrew scriptures, the desert experience begins with a man who had a son. But Abraham cannot talk to his son any more than he can talk to his sheep. His son is always of a different time and a different place ("Go from your native land and your father's house"). The son cannot feel what is in the father's heart—he is too young and too distant from what his father experiences. Abraham is a nomad: To whom could he release the fearful burden of his heart? Who would understand? But his intense loneliness allows him to hear, from across the world of silence, the call that will ever after give meaning to all things.

The Egyptians were not willing to wait for the call. They read meaning in bird entrails and animal bones, and demanded that the silent objects of the world speak to their concerns. The Egyptians' world became thick with their own meanings, drowning out forever their intrinsic silence. Yet silence is a good, even essential component of reality, allowing us to discover rather than create the meaning underlying appearance. The Egyptians unleashed the noise of omens and portents, drowning out their own thoughts. Moses led the Children of Israel into the wilderness to experience silence once more.

After the first excitement of liberation from Egypt, the Israelites had to be liberated not merely *from* slavery but *to* some deeper awareness of freedom. The desert is a difficult place in which to construct reality, but that is precisely what we are called to do. As former slaves, the Israelites needed ways of centering and organizing. "One such way of 'centering,' of recalling a self, . . . can be given by music, by art of all kinds."[3] The music of the Song at the Sea was one important example of this new centering, but no less significant was the music of time unfolding in structured ways. With the wilderness of space, the Children of Israel needed a structuredness of time—hence the recurring Sabbath and the recurring hours of prayer. Within each day there were fixed hours of prayer, within each week the day of Sabbath, within each month the festival of the new moon, and within each year the round of holy days. Unstructured space was balanced by highly structured time.

In the desert, the Israelites required community and love to insure their continued sanity. "The merciless sensation of the coldness of space, of the vast void out there, was intensified by the absolute stillness of the desert night until it became inhuman, unbearable. . . . We, the living, were linked in the face of . . . the cruel coldness of the universe and the emptiness of the desert around us."[4] It was, in part, this immense loneliness that led to the formation of a unified people.

We let go of community to see what no one has seen. We form our own values, which are not yet fully defined, outside cultural structures. Seeking a precedent, we might look at how Judaism was formed. Perhaps it began with Moses, who needed others to share his unique vision. But even before Moses, Abraham was called to leave his home and his father's house to see what had not been seen before. Abraham needed a family to sustain his vision; that is why fathering a son was so crucial to him, something that was less important to Moses. Moses would not be content to pass on his faith through the slow process of generations, he had to transform the Children of Israel within his own lifetime. In his final address to the Israelites, Moses foretells their fall from faith. The importance of his prediction—and what differentiates his vision from those of others—is that it does not depend on him personally. The religion is not Moses', but God's, so even if Moses fails to pass it on, revelation will continue nevertheless to work its way throughout history. It is, on reflection, not Moses' vision but God's revelation that the Hebrew scriptures describe.

Moses does not have the revelation at the burning bush for his own sake but for the sake of the Israelites and, ultimately, for all the world. Moses cannot simply describe his vision—God's revelation—to the people, but must somehow transmit the revelation that had so transformed his life. The Israelites needed to shed their way of understanding reality, a task that is always difficult. If our personal quest for truth is now understood as experiencing God's revelation, then we need not mold our children; rather, we must be faithful to the emerging truth and know that it will continue to work its way throughout history.

The time in the wilderness is spent instructing the people in new categories: sacred and profane, Sabbath and weekdays, Israel and other nations. The categories were initially formulated dualistically, although a deeper understanding would develop over time. The Israelites had to refashion the world in their own way, creating structures in the light of their shared experiences. They create these structures only by remembering, naming, and teaching their experiences, thereby helping create and unify the people. Once their old world was shed, a new one could emerge. Constructing a tabernacle in the wilderness was an exercise in world building. The Children of Israel and each of us will have many desert experiences. We must look at these experiences carefully to discover how they function and what creativity is embedded within our deepest trials.

The desert is a geographical place, but it is also a metaphorical place—of emptiness, unchartedness, loneliness—that describes many aspects of the human condition. The musical equivalent of the desert would be silence, from which the new song will come forth. The song of the slave, which accompanied the servitude under Pharaoh, is silenced. Silence does not initially feel relieving or even neutral because we associate it with God's absence or distance from our lives. Before we can discover the song welling up from within, we must purge the old song. Before we can enter into a healing silence, we must experience the terror that wells up out of the initial silence.

Silence in its simplest form is the absence of speech. The steps to silence are learned in the desert. We carry noise around with us. Even after the outer noise has been quieted, the inner noise remains. Eventually, even that becomes stilled, and it is then that we discover the intimate relationship between silence and terror. Noise serves as an important distraction that keeps us from facing the many dangers within. Silence forces us to confront our fears, allowing us finally to reach quietness, repose, and a wholeness within.

The first door that silence opens is a gateway to terrifying memories. For the Children of Israel the first terror in the wilderness comes in the form of the pursuing Egyptians. While this fear is initially grounded in reality, it remains as an unreal threat long after the real Egyptians are gone. Next, memory becomes distorted, and the harsh years of servitude are remembered as the "fleshpots of Egypt." The power of the Egyptians, as a pursuing army or as a tempting memory, lies in the consciousness of the Israelites. They alone invest the Egyptians with power, and they alone can withdraw it. Since reality can be defined as that which has power to affect, the Egyptians were real to some of the Israelites and not to others. Upon entering into silence, we, like the Israelites, confront first the conflicts in our lives. We might compare this situation to diving into the ocean and finding first the flotsam and jetsam floating on top—the terrors on the surface—and then going deeper and finding the terrors in the depths, and then going even deeper into the dark stillness.

Shortly after their entry into the wilderness, the Israelites come down with plague. Illness affords them yet another way of examining their identity by teaching them their dependence on others. Illness restricts their view of identity by restricting their vision of possibilities. But illness can also be crucial to growth. In experiencing illness, we discover that the boundary of self has become a semipermeable membrane. In illness we cannot afford the boundaries between self and other that we so frequently erect when we are well, because illness forces us to extend our boundaries to include our caregivers. During our brief moments of illness, we experience the possibility of widening our definition of self.

Illness can be understood in two ways: as a foreign body (bacterium or virus) entering our own body, or as a breakdown of our immune system. In this second view, germs are necessary but not sufficient to explain illness. Neither of these scientific or medical models takes the relationship between illness and identity seriously. We tend to treat a health breakdown the way we treat a car breakdown, by taking our body in for repairs. But we should have learned in the desert that vulnerability is part of being human. The desert hints that context influences health and that we are affected and infected by what is around us, whether it is germs or fears. Illness shows us some of our vulnerabilities and dependencies, causing us to ask what reality must be like if this is happening. The vulnerabilities of illness are tied up with loss and grieving. Illness, like other losses, indicates to us that our sense of self is too limited and our life plan must be rethought. Part of that rethinking consists of trying to make sense of getting sick.

The Children of Israel must also face attack in the wilderness. Wars and illness can be understood in similar ways. We can use the external model of illness to explain war, that is, invasion by a foreign body, or the internal model, that is, breakdown of the system. Indeed, war can be viewed as a form of illness writ large. The internal view of war suggests that there are tendencies within the self that make one liable to war. We are not attuned to what the body (politic) needs. Living tissue is flexible, but we are not flexible enough, and the worst rigidity we can suffer is hardness of the heart. In order to kill, we have to wound ourselves in a serious way: we have to harden our hearts, that is, bring on a diseased condition. We must deform ourselves in order to undertake war.

The Children of Israel confronted the power of the Egyptians, a nameable fear, but they also had to deal with anxieties that emerged in the silence. Nameable fears are less wild than anxieties, which do not submit to names. Anxieties are experiences of raw terror untamed by reason or causality. The answer to terror is not to fight it or reason with it but to accept it. A terror accepted is a terror transformed. Gradually, out of the terror of the wilderness will emerge the beginnings of joy.

The same desert that brought the Israelites haunting memories, fear, anxiety, vulnerability, and war also brought them revelation, because the desert of aloneness is also a center for creativity and the life force. Avoiding solitude means cutting ourselves off from creativity. We need to see what the desert holds and accept it on its own terms, because at its heart the desert is alive, fruitful, and energizing.

As Walter Kaufmann explains it, the Children of Israel learned in the desert that

> the sacred is here and now. The only God worth keeping is a God that cannot be kept. The only God worth talking about is a God that cannot be talked about. God is no object of discourse, knowledge, or even experience. He cannot be spoken of, but he can be spoken to; he cannot be seen, but he can be listened to. The only possible relationship with God is to address him and to be addressed by him, here and now—or, as Buber puts it, in the present. For him the Hebrew name of God, the tetragrammaton (YHVH), means HE IS PRESENT.[5]

For the Children of Israel, the sojourn in the desert was a time to confront their physical vulnerability to disease, hunger, and attack. It was a time to face the unresolved issues of memory and unnamed fears. And it was a time of revelation, in the form of the Ten Words (Commandments) given at Mount Sinai. The first content of the revelation at Sinai is Presence. An awareness by the Israelites of God's presence restructured their memory so that they could be healed from bitterness and empowered to right social wrongs. These were the Ten Words that came forth from Sinai (Exod. 20:2–14):

I the Lord am your God who brought you out of the land of Egypt, the house of bondage.

These words clearly affirm to the Children of Israel that everything they had experienced—water turning into blood, epidemics of frogs and lice, their hasty flight from Egypt, their terror at the sea, the parting of the waters—was planned and meaningful. From the moment of Moses' return to Egypt, all had occurred not by chance but through God's loving care. How reassuring for the Israelites to look back at past events and realize that God had been with them and for them all along. The lash and brickworks of Egypt were not forgotten, but the dominant memory was now a larger awareness of God's presence and concern.

You shall have no other gods beside Me.

Everything now arranged itself in terms of this ordering. A

sense of wonder was growing, a sense of beauty and love.

You shall not swear falsely by the name of the Lord your God.

God's name is Presence, present through all that the Israelites had experienced, present in the Word that was being given, and present in the words they would utter. By awareness of Presence, of the holy, we can "guard [our] tongue from evil, [our] lips from deceitful speech" (Ps. 34:14).

Remember the Sabbath day and keep it holy.

The Sabbath is a way of carrying the desert experience with us. In the desert, the structuredness of time (thrice-daily prayers, the weekly Sabbath, the monthly new moon) helped tame the wilderness. But in the structure of our settled state, the Sabbath provides an opportunity to return to the many doors of silence and to non-domesticated time. Buber speaks of prayer as being "not in time but time in prayer, the sacrifice not in space but space in the sacrifice—and whoever reverses the relation annuls the reality. ... As long as the firmament of the You is spread over me, the tempests of causality cower at my heels, and the whirl of doom congeals."[6] In the desert of time, on the Sabbath, we release control. We release the principles of causality by which we manipulate and shape our reality, and experience the gift of Creation. In this desert of time and space, we are open to revelation.

Honor your father and your mother.

The fourth of the Ten Words arises naturally from the earlier statements. Families challenge us all. But Judaism makes clear that we can arrive at universal love only through particular love we have for those people in our lives. To draw an analogy: we may learn many languages during our lifetime but we need to begin with one language that we learn well—well enough to intuit the deep structure of the language, the possibility for metaphor, simile, and poetry. And while we may study many religions, we need to go beyond the literal level to the level of metaphor, simile, and poetry by dwelling long enough in one religion to develop a comfort with its structure and an ease with its form. There is one family in which we have been set down. We need to learn well its strengths and its weaknesses, as well as our own strengths and weaknesses in relation to its members. Most of Genesis is concerned with working out family relationships, because that is one of our central human tasks. How we see "the other," be it father, mother, or sibling, ultimately determines how we see ourselves. The self that sees the other simply as that which opposes us or needs to be controlled by us is constricted. Transforming our view of the other transforms our view of the self, and changing our understanding of the self transforms our relationship to others. Behind the other who is our parent or sibling is the other who is God. As our image of God expands, so does our image of self. We are created in the image of God.

You shall not murder.

This Word follows fast on the heels of "honor your father and your mother," for our most murderous thoughts attach themselves to those closest to us. From Cain and Abel onward, those near to us have seemed most threatening to our being. In discovering that family members are not simply what they are in relationship to ourselves but are people in their own right, we expand our notion of them and release any need to control or strike out.

You shall not commit adultery.

Working through the concept of otherness has shown us our infinite worth and the other's infinite worth. We cannot respect the mystery that is our self and dishonor another. We begin to sense that in and through the mysteries of the self and the other is the deeper mystery of God. We are created in God's image, and we see imaged in the covenant with our spouse the Israelites' covenant with God. "Metaphors for God both shape and are shaped by our life experiences, especially our most significant relationships."[7] Our faithfulness to God shines through the faithfulness to our spouse.

You shall not steal.

We have learned in the desert that the world before we have "tamed" it is gift enough for our being and well-being. Stealing is motivated by lack of trust—there won't be enough for us all. But trust has been growing, so we need not steal or grasp.

You shall not bear false witness against your neighbor.

We cannot hurt the other without damaging the self.

You shall not covet.

Our growing trust, our experience of giftedness, our awareness of God's presence and concern, and our knowledge that the self is inextricably connected to the other have changed the shape of our hopes and dreams. We cannot covet.

Sinai was a revelation of beauty—of wholeness, inner coherence, fitness. "To the religious, natural beauty suggests divine wisdom."[8] The effect of this experience of beauty was pleasure and love.

The Children of Israel gained their strongest experience of the desert following the Exodus from Egypt, but their descendants also experienced wandering, the breakdown of familiar borders, and entry into the unknown. Periodically we experience the awesome sojourn in the desert and find ourselves facing the uncharted experiences of vulnerability and confusion. We take heart in remembering that central to the desert experience is revelation, and we remain open to the revelation inherent in our own deserts.

6 | *Aging*

Aging puts us through the trials of the desert all over again. We must finally lay to rest the ghosts of our past and face up to our vulnerability and mortality. So aging is a natural route to enlightenment. Another path to awareness is taken by mystics, whose disciplines force them to confront finitude and interdependence. Actually, the disciplines of the spiritual life accelerate the natural growth of awareness so that those who choose the spiritual life can live for a longer time in close relationship to reality.

Part of our quest for the self is active, but quieter kinds of activity are also required: waiting, suffering, experiencing, and remaining open through all that happens to us. Built into the normal trajectory of a life are many of the processes that will transform our sense of self and otherness; the central one is aging and, with it, our growing awareness of death.

As the basis for a historical religion, the Hebrew scriptures teach us that God's will and meaning are revealed through events in time: large events, such as the Exodus from Egypt, the conquest of the Promised Land, and the rise of the Davidic kingdom, and also smaller events, such as the way time tempers many of the central figures—Jacob, Joseph, Moses, and ourselves. The Bible assures us that our lives are not just one day after another, but that the days flow into one another, forming a pattern that is itself revelation. If we take time seriously, we should also take the regular pattern of time in our lives seriously. It then becomes crucial to ask, Who must we be and what must life mean that aging is part of the normal life process? The theologian John S. Dunne dwells on this question:

Now if there were a man who never dismissed a fact of his experience as a mere coincidence, he would have difficulty taking in stride the facts which regularly occur in human lives. The regular occurrence of a fact would not constitute an explanation in his eyes. For instance a young man, let us say, is confronted with the fact that men grow old, take sick, and die, and that this will eventually happen to him too, though he is now young and healthy and alive. If he is accustomed to finding significance and appropriateness in the coincidences of his life, in the persons he meets, in the course events take, in the words that are spoken to him, in the thoughts that occur to him, he is likely to look for significance and appropriateness also in these other facts of his life. . . . The prospect of sickness, old age, and death will make it impossible to continue living as before and will make it seem necessary to enter upon a new way.[1]

We learn from the biblical stories that time makes a difference. Time is real, though not ultimate, and revelation takes place in and through time. History—personal and national—is an accounting of transformations. By looking back, we gain some perspective on the distance we have traveled and realize that we were not born completed. "A human being is not there all at once in a moment; to be human takes time and involves development."[2] We grow and are changed by our experiences and choices. We are in process, and we are a process. What we see in the story of Jacob we see as clearly in our own lives.

The portrayal of aging in Genesis provides a way to deal with the spirituality of later life. Abraham experiences the loss of his wife and comes to recognize that he too must die. He then cares for the ongoingness of time by arranging Isaac's marriage. Isaac feigns senility as Jacob "steals" Esau's blessing, but then lives another twenty years. His apparent weakness is essential if Jacob is to experience his own emerging strength. Jacob, in his Testament, looks over his whole life in what the psychologist Erik Erikson would name "integrity" and expresses his values through his predictions for his sons. Joseph identifies with a time when he will no longer be and asks that his bones be carried out when a future generation leaves Egypt.

Each of our individual lives, considered over its full expanse, can be considered a revelation, and we should not be surprised that the development of the characters in Genesis resembles the development within our own life: we may begin as Abraham and end as Joseph.

At the end of Joseph's life, we see his sense of integrity. For him to have become the person he became, he must see all that preceded as inevitable. That is not to rule out free will: in prospect our choices are freely made, and we are responsible. In retrospect we see the meaning inherent in the choices we made and feel that they could not have been otherwise. According to Evelyn Eaton Whitehead and James D. Whitehead, Erikson

> calls this mature stage, the full fruit of human development, integrity. Understood as a resource of the mature personality, integrity is seen in "the acceptance of one's one and only life cycle and of the people who have become significant to it as something that had to be, and that, by necessity, permitted no substitutions."... It is rather an affirmation of the "givenness"—the inevitability—of my own life's course. This sense of inevitability comes in retrospect. It is rooted in an acceptance of the goodness of *now*. Because I accept myself and my meaning now, I can look back to salute the drama of pain and joy that has brought me to this point.[3]

This interconnectedness of freedom and destiny is spelled out further by Martin Buber:

> Free is the man that wills without caprice. He believes in the actual, which is to say: he believes in the real association of the real duality, I and You. He believes in destiny and also that it needs him. It does not lead him, it waits for him.... He must go forth with his whole being.[4]

We can view Job's life as we can our own—as a trajectory. We begin at birth, arrive through education, growth, and numerous experiences at full individuation, and then begin the slow decline into old age and death. Are we really ourselves only at the pinnacle, or is the self there at birth and just as fully there during old age? If we are ourselves at every moment of this journey, then who or what is the self, and how does the process of aging make manifest what is hidden? But perhaps we have misdescribed the entire trajectory. Life is not primarily a movement from dependence to increasing independence back to dependence, or a movement of ascent that reverses direction and ends with descent into death. Certainly loss and diminishment accompany aging. Aging is a process of change, and all change entails the loss of what was before and the gain of what is now. Contemporary Western society tends to emphasize the loss accompanying aging. The Mishnah, on the other hand, emphasizes the gain: "They stood up in prayer and sent down before the Ark an old man, well versed in prayer, one that had children and whose house was empty of sustenance, so that he might be whole-hearted in the prayer."[5] There is the sense that aging, raising a family, and living through the joys and sorrows of these processes enable us to pray with fewer distractions and more fervor. Aging can be a process of simplification, in which we release the complexities of our society, its roles, and its rituals. We release the busyness and frenetic social activity and can simply be. The writer May Sarton describes old age as an ascension. "The ascension is possible when all that has to be given up can be *gladly* given up—because other things have become more important."[6] We can also think about aging in terms of creativity and destruction. We create selves that must be destroyed so that new selves can emerge.

We have looked at various characters in Genesis to see how they age, but we could also view the Bible as telling the story of a single life through all of its characters. Rabbi Hillel's statement quoted in *The Ethics of the Fathers* gives us an excellent way to begin:

If I am not for myself, who will be for me?
And if I am only for myself what am I?
And if not now, when?[7]

Dunne interprets this statement to mean that we must first have a self before we can give it up.[8] Abraham's story is the paradigm for the formation of the self. His is a life shaped by defining the self in terms of radical difference and separation that reaches its climax in a personal encounter with God. Abraham is first separated from his nation and kindred, then from his nephew, finally even from his sons. What remains is a direct, unmediated relationship to God, divorced from any human interaction. This direct approach to God may account for Abraham's seeming inhumanity in his willingness to send Ishmael into the wilderness with only one skin of water and his readiness to sacrifice his son Isaac. Abraham's awareness of self represents a major turning point in human spiritual growth. Until Abraham could recognize his selfhood—that he existed separate and distinct from his surroundings—he could not emerge from the world of his idol-worshipping ancestors to search for and ultimately come into relationship with God. He could not begin to question the values he took from his surroundings until he could recognize that he was distinct from his surroundings and thereby in a position to examine and evaluate the local beliefs. But because the concept of self was then so newly acquired, its boundaries are not expressed clearly in Genesis. We cannot be entirely sure where Abraham ends and his sons begin: Are they property to be sacrificed, aspects of the self to be nurtured, or "the other" against which Abraham must measure and define himself? Abraham's God, however, is radically other—the one who speaks through the awesome theophanies of the Covenant between the Pieces (Gen. 15:2–21), the destruction of Sodom and Gomorrah, and the Binding of Isaac.

From Abraham's pivotal acquisition of self, the biblical account turns first to Isaac, whose self-knowledge is kindled by the loss of his mother and the comfort provided by his bride, and then to Jacob, whose complex family history activates the drama of Joseph and his brothers. That Joseph's story occupies fully one-quarter of the Book of Genesis suggests its importance. Joseph resembles us in a significant way: he has no direct experience of God. He knows God only by inference from his experiences and from his own insights into those experiences. He must discover God in and through the events of his life, much as we must discern the working of God in the day-to-day events of our lives. The story of Joseph begins with the differentiated love Jacob feels for his two wives and two concubines. Perhaps it begins even earlier, in Jacob's feelings of guilt about stealing his father's blessing from his brother. It is impossible to think of Joseph without thinking of his brothers, and once we think about them, we are thrown back to a long troubled history of sibling relationships in Genesis: Cain and Abel, Ishmael and Isaac, Jacob and Esau, Rachel and Leah. The mundaneness through which Joseph finds God—not on a mountain but in reconciling with his family—is an important element in Genesis. Joseph heals his relationship with his brothers and with his father, and that healing is his way to God. When the dying Joseph extracts a promise from his descendants— "When God has taken notice of you, you shall carry up my bones from here" (Gen. 50:25)—he leaps forward in his imagination to a time of Israel's deliverance and asks to be a party to it. By identifying his fate not with his own limited and personal being but with that of his people, Joseph transcends the events that occur to him personally and achieves the long perspective that allows him to discern God's working through his life.

From Exodus through Deuteronomy, Moses serves as the central character. His two sons hardly figure in the story because they are no more likely to follow in his way than are any other young men of that time. In meeting God face to face, Moses comes to recognize and appreciate God's celebration of diversity and of freedom—love freely given—so, unlike Abraham and Jacob, who molded their sons, Moses does not.

The quest for the self is not a steady forward movement. Along with the expanding concept of self come our experiences of the losses we face in life, as exemplified in the Book of Lamentations. Our necessary losses are spelled out in the parable of aging found in the Book of Ecclesiastes (which closely resembles the description of the deserted city in Lamentations):

> When the guards of the house become shaky,
> And the men of valor are bent,
> And the maids that grind, grown few, are idle,
> And the ladies that peer through the windows grow dim,
> And the doors to the street are shut—
> With the noise of the hand mill growing fainter,
> And the song of the bird growing feebler,
> And all the strains of music dying down;
> When one is afraid of heights
> And there is terror on the road.—
> For the almond tree may blossom,
> The grasshopper be burdened,
> And the caper bush may bud again;
> But man sets out for his eternal abode,
> With mourners all around in the street.—
> Before the silver cord snaps
> And the golden bowl crashes,
> The jar is shattered at the spring,
> And the jug is smashed at the cistern.
> And the dust returns to the ground
> As it was,
> And the lifebreath returns to God
> Who bestowed it.
>
> (Eccles. 12:3–7)

This allegory of age, while powerful, is not the Bible's last word on the subject. The Book of Job brings us face to face with the doubts behind all our successes and with a final perspective on self. Job is not exceptional, he is Everyman. His universality shows us our vulnerability and confusion before our inevitable losses and experiences of injustice. We must ask, then, who Job is at the *end* of the Book of Job: How is his concept of self related to those of Abraham, Isaac, Jacob, Joseph, Moses, Jeremiah, and Ecclesiastes?

The Book of Job, which can be read as expressing a fully developed self, appears at first to explain the self by radically stripping away its surface levels of wealth, status, relationships, even bodily integrity. If, like Job, we begin with the view that since life is meaningful its trajectory must have meaning also, then our lack of self-understanding compels us to join in Job's cry through all these changes, "Let something remain!" And if Job portrays a vision of our own aging, then the aging process can be seen as the stripping away of an identity built up over many years, consisting of the physical self, the rational self, and the emotional self. Let something remain. How different our world looks to us when we are starting out and when we look back. We spend a long part of our lives building up a self and spend the rest of our lives tearing it down. What is built and what is destroyed?

In the Book of Job, the essential action is not tearing down Job's self but opening it up to a new vision of reality. Paradoxically, the movement begun by loss is one that expands. The Book of Job speaks to us not only because Job precipitously loses what we all lose in the process of aging—status, jobs, identity, physical health, those we love—but because it gives account of what Job gains: the transformation of the self, as portrayed in the theophany.

Job's earlier self is understood in the context of his friends. But although his relationships with his friends form part of his self-understanding, they do not complete it, as we see when his friends challenge his basic perception. Their refusal to empathize with him constitutes one of Job's greatest trials and, paradoxically, a significant means for him to enter his expanded concept of self.

Both attempts by Bildad, one of Job's comforters, to answer Job's problems turn on the concept of time. His first response is that we should look to history for an answer to the problem of evil. He suggests that a single person's lifetime is not an adequate perspective from which to view good and evil, and that each lifetime must be viewed within the context of the whole people. Bildad's response in no way contradicts what we saw in our own examination of memory (chapter 4). He is not wrong, he is just not right. Bildad's second response is that the brevity of our life is inadequate for genuine knowledge, that we are ephemeral and know nothing. That argument is related to the first but is not identical with it. His response confirms what we already saw in

Genesis 1: we are limited by the other creatures of Creation, by other humans, and by our own finitude. If we are alive but briefly, is there anything we can know?

We often feel that there is something we don't know that leads to the problem of evil, that if we could know and understand, we would see how everything fits together and makes acceptable sense. Perhaps we do know, but know incorrectly. We have eaten from the Tree but have not properly digested the fruit. There must be a species of knowledge that could heal both Job and us.

The theophany (Job 38–41) expresses eloquently God's response to Job's challenge. Let us leave aside two millennia of interpretation and simply enter into these lines.

Who is this who darkens counsel
Speaking without knowledge?
(38:2)

Knowledge has been the problem from Genesis 3 onward. There is a knowledge that gives life and a knowledge that is opposed to the Tree of Life. Life-giving knowledge connects us to what we know, uniting the knower and the known. The knowledge opposed to the Tree of Life is what distinguishes us from or sets us in opposition to all else.

Where were you when I laid the earth's foundations?
(38:4)

This question can be understood on several levels. If we are not aware of the design, we are not in a position to judge it. Our absence in the beginning suggests that we really have an imperfect perspective for evaluating Creation. The question, however, says more: it is an invitation to go experientially back with God to how it was in the beginning—to experience the joy God has in Creation. It also serves as an appeal to return to the primordial darkness and undifferentiated being that underlie our own creative process. The complex relationship between our self-conscious awareness of our own creative process and our awareness of the role Job's trials played in his life is not spelled out in the theophany; rather, Job is invited merely to touch on the experience of going back to the beginning as a possible source for his own answer.

Do you know who fixed its dimensions
Or who measured it with a line?
(38:5)

The text is set up as a series of questions to evoke responses in Job. Job must search within himself for answers, discover his own inadequacies, and so move on to transcendence. The question reminds Job how deeply God loves creation. God's care is spelled out, from the fundamental proportions and measurements to the fine details.

> Onto what were its bases sunk?
> Who set its corner-stone
> When the morning stars sang together
> And all the divine beings shouted for joy?
> (38:6)

The imagery is of joy in creation. To be is to be good! In Spinoza's words, "By reality and perfection I understand the same thing." As Job confronts God about his pain, God refocuses Job's attention on the goodness of Creation. "Let them praise the name of the Lord; for he commanded and they were created. He fixed them fast forever and ever; he gave a law which none transgresses" (Ps. 148:5). Built into the notion of Creation are limits and boundaries, and the rest of creation knows and respects their place. But people who are less aware that all being interconnects bump up against the limits and are less likely to praise the name of the Lord. To praise God is to be, and to be what you are most fully.

> Have you penetrated to the sources of the sea
> Or walked in the recesses of the deep?
> (38:16)

This line suggests two meanings: Have we entered into our own source? This return into our own self, into our inner source of being and nourishment, is an experiential response to the quest for meaning. The text also invites us to reflect on the primordial waters prior to their division on the second day of Creation. The waters above the heavens *are* the waters below; there is no difference in material, only in perception.

> Have the gates of death been disclosed to you?
> (38:17)

God responds to Job's experience of evil by focusing instead on the joy inherent in creation. But since God does address death, the problem of death cannot be conflated with the problem of evil. Only when we see death as a part of life and not as its opposite, only when we move beyond duality, can we heal Job's wounds.

Which path leads to where light dwells,
And where is the place of darkness . . . ?
(38:19)

"Who forms light and creates darkness." Again, we must go
beyond dualistic thinking and recognize the single source of light
and darkness.

To rain down on uninhabited land,
On the wilderness where no man is, . . .
(38:26)

People are not the center of the creation. God's concern extends
beyond any single being to being itself; so must Job's.

Can you hunt prey for the lion,
And satisfy the appetite of the king of beasts?
(38:39)

The text continues to emphasize a perspective that extends
beyond a concern for humans to a concern for all being. Focusing
on undomesticated animals challenges our presumed place at the
center of the universe. Job 39 describes various wild beasts and
God's concern for them: hind, wild ass (onager), wild ox, ostrich,
horse, hawk, eagle. This emphasis continues with elaborate
descriptions of Behemoth (40:15–24) and Leviathan (40:25–32).

God gives Job at least four answers in the theophany. Job asks
if there is divine providence. God answers by simply speaking to
Job. The theologian Thomas Merton finds that answer enough,
holding that if God cares enough to communicate, then there is
divine providence.[9] God's second answer, given to the comforters, is, "You have not spoken the truth about Me as did My
servant Job" (42:7). Job's great dismay is brought on in part by the
comforters' challenging Job's view of reality. God's answer
affirms Job's, so Job can be comforted. God's third answer
appears in the speech of Elihu, a young man who joins the con-
versation after the comforters have spoken. Although the passage
is often dismissed as a later interpolation, it curiously mirrors
God's own speech.

God's fourth answer can be formulated by using a distinction
drawn by Bernard of Clairvaux. Bernard distinguishes four stages
of love: (1) you are to love yourself (harder to do than Bernard
thinks and should not, perhaps, be listed first); (2) you are to love
God for the sake of the self (an instrumental view, which is in fact
the view that Satan accuses Job of holding [1:9]); (3) you are to

love God for the sake of God (what many people think the Book of Job is about—the quest for the disinterested love for God); and (4) you are to love yourself for the sake of God (what the Book of Job really is about and why it provides insight into the process of aging).

The eye (read also "I") is blind because it cannot see itself. God invites Job—and us—to see ourselves from God's perspective, allowing us at last to feel God's joy in creation and to experience true self-acceptance. Identifying with all of being allows Job to transcend his personal suffering. And, according to Robert Grudin, "we can attempt the even more profound renewal, available I think only to the old, of partially shedding our individual selves and participating in a grander social and biological identity."[10] The Book of Job does not end with justice, which Job originally seeks, but rather with love, which satisfies him beyond his original quest.

We have viewed change over time as a refiner's fire, in which something is transformed and brought more closely to its essential nature. But what of the final change, death? Is that a refiner's fire or a holocaust? Can something live through that change? Kathleen Fischer has observed, "At every point in the human journey we find that we have to let go in order to move forward; and letting go means dying a little."[11] But how is "dying a little" like dying? Is there a quantitative difference—all of our little deaths are preparation for death—or a qualitative difference— nothing persists through this ultimate change? If we take seriously the collapsing of dualisms that we have traced, the sense that nothing is absolutely set off and opposed, then death is one more stage in a unified process. "A single 'Yes!' goes through the whole of life. It is successively 'Yes!' to childhood, to youth, to adult life, to old age, and finally 'Yes!' to death."[12]

Death is a stage in the process of self. "That man is ephemeral is the beginning of wisdom, not its end. . . . Each of us is as ephemeral as the grass in the field, but there is no point in dwelling on that; there is work to be done."[13] While biblical thought does not focus on death, it is not denied. The major figures plan for their "gathering to their ancestors" but do not cry out against death. The Bible focuses instead on "the work to be done." Along with a belief in the meaningfulness of life—the only stance that makes death acceptable—comes a belief that we have a task to perform. Like our biblical counterparts, we believe we have some unique perspective or skill to contribute to the larger whole. Elisabeth Kübler-Ross comments in her study of the dying how grateful they are that they can still contribute something. She suggests that what we most need is a place where we can give.[14]

Our central concern should not be "how to escape death, but rather how to sanctify life." Our participation in the work of the world transforms our relationship to death. In our efforts to heal the world we come into the Presence. In our sacred use of time we experience eternity, because "eternity is not perpetual future but perpetual presence."[15] A life lived with touches of eternity conditions us to hope—not for some specific image of afterlife, but hope in God who was present, is present, and will be present.

7 | *Quest for the Self*

As we explore the development of the self, we begin to recognize that something is missing in the Western notion of self: "As man came to realize himself as 'autonomous man,' he left out the most essential component of his being, namely the factor of 'love,' which is inseparable from freedom and equality in the existence of religious man."[1] We see that because of God's love, the world comes to us organized not simply through space and time but through beauty, the song of our consciousness. God's love allows us to identify so with our song that we develop the freedom to improvise, to be creative. And we recognize that love breaks down the otherness of the other and allows us to see the shared role we play in the whole. We have seen God's love but have not recognized our own. Our capacity to love and our need to be nourished by others' love suggests that "autonomy" is not as central to our existence as interconnection. We are drawn back to the love that surrounds us in and through the beauty of our world.

Our world is made up of time and space (context) and some principle of organization. From the biblical perspective, the world comes to us organized by the principle of beauty, but what about the other two components, time and space? According to Maurice Maeterlinck, "It were much more reasonable to persuade ourselves that the catastrophes which we think that we behold are life itself, the joy and one or other of those immense festivals of mind and matter in which death, *thrusting aside at last our two enemies, time and space,* will soon permit us to take part"(emphasis added).[2] The view that time and space are unreal or inimical prevails in some philosophies. Judaism and the Judaic-based religions reject this view. Time is believed to be real, though not ultimate. It is subject to our consciousness and our actions, and well-chosen actions can lift the temporal into the eternal: "Eternity is not perpetual future but perpetual presence. . . . This is the meaning of existence: to reconcile liberty with service, the passing with the lasting, to weave the threads of temporality into the fabric of eternity."[3]

Space is also considered real but not ultimate. Our particular history, the time and place in which we have been set, is regarded as meaningful. Our individuality and uniqueness are, again, real if not ultimate. We cannot love universally: we can love only those people we find in our particular time and space. We discover that love transcends time and space (and, according to the Song of Songs, it is fiercer than death), but we discover that only after we have learned to love real, particular people. Judaism takes time, change, and history seriously, and stresses that time is subject to our consciousness. Historical religions educate their followers about time. They combine historical time (commemorating important events in the story of the people) with "pre"-historical events (celebrating such occasions as the "birthday of the world"—Rosh Hashanah) and experiences of the eternal in time (the weekly Sabbath). Devotees become aware of how their participation helps to form the event. For example, every Friday evening observant Jews "make" Sabbath, that is, declare that Sabbath has begun. Although Sabbath is real and independent of the participants, they must still be attentive and consciously bring it into being.

In addition to affirming the reality of time and space, Judaism makes clear that while we must transform the self, the transformation does not end with the "no-self" that we find in some Eastern thought. The self remains the center out of which we come into relationship with God and with the family. But the transformed self is no longer defined narrowly in terms of the self in opposition, it is the self in relatedness.

The otherness that is played out in the story of Cain and Abel reappears in the stories of Isaac and Ishmael, Sarah and Hagar, Esau and Jacob, and Rachel and Leah. The story of Joseph and his brothers takes a different turn. At first, Joseph's brothers form an undifferentiated group aligned in their enmity toward him. But differences among them emerge and changes take place in their lives and attitudes because time has an effect. When the full story is played out, it is not Joseph's line that emerges as the primary historical root but the line of his brother Judah. Multiplicity is real—the brothers become more and more differentiated—but otherness is not absolute.

The psychologist Joanna Field writes, "When Adam and Eve ate of the tree of knowledge, did that mean becoming self-conscious? They also became aware of shame, of inferiority; with becoming aware of self, they also became aware of 'not self.'" In fact, it is probably through focusing on the other, the "not-self," that they become aware of the self because, in Walter Kaufmann's words, "consciousness precedes self-consciousness, and we become aware of the deeds and behavior of others before we become aware of our own." Field asks whether it is possible "to become self-conscious, to eat of the tree of knowledge of good and evil without also becoming paralyzed with shame and the sense of one's own smallness."[4]

We associate self-consciousness with discomfort and unease. We tend to notice something—the foot, the heart—when it is not working right, but when it is well, it escapes our attention. So it is with the self, but the self usually is not working right, thereby obstructing our free, unself-conscious use of it. We should aim, then, to cease focusing on the self in order to be free simply to use it. The self is not unreal, it should just not be the object of our consciousness. If we learn to get the self "out of the way," we can become one with what we wish to learn.

The Eastern philosophies that advocate "no-self" do not recognize a distinction between the self and our consciousness of the self. Not being conscious of the self is not the same as not having a self.[5] A pianist who no longer pays conscious attention to the separate motions of the fingers is not someone who no longer has fingers, but someone whose fingers function so well that the consciousness can focus entirely on the music. When we finally "get out of the way," our consciousness can focus on the music around us.

We not only have a self, in the process of living we become aware of a multiplicity of selves. At times of creativity or intuition, something seems to be living through us, or, as Freud wrote, "I am lived." This force within ourselves is not our conscious self. The psychoanalyst Marion Milner, writing about this phenomenon, comes to trust this self and calls it the deeper self. She strives to shift her identity from the conscious self to this deeper self, which she identifies as the source of her creativity. We all discover, when trying to make a decision, that we have more than a single voice. How can we find our truest voice?

In our quest for the self, we must first become fully who we are, as Rabbi Hillel implies: "If I am not for myself, who will be for me?" Only when we have integrated the many aspects of the self can we undertake the next step, disintegrating the boundaries of the self: "If I am only for myself, what am I?" We now begin to realize that the self is a process that points to something more enduring. It is not the end product but the means by which we get to the end product or, put another way, we are not our own goal. We are willing contributors to a goal that is larger than our own life and effort. We are a part of the whole, like a voice in a choir, but even if we are lost in the whole we still have an individual role to play. Job finds, after the theophany, the self that gives rise to spontaneous right action and creativity. He has let go of the constricted sense of self and so lets go of both fear and suffering.

Our quest for the self is a process of changing the place where we locate ourselves. Our younger self was closely identified with physical being. When we are older, we are less aware of our physical self, except when we are hurt. Ideally, we want to use our physical self without thinking about it. Similarly, we want to use our entire self rather than think about it. The biblical texts suggest ways of understanding our experiences. The experiences themselves are not as important as the transformation that results from understanding them.

The transformative process in Job begins by negation: we are not our physical being. That does not mean that we take no responsibility for how we appear, but it suggests that we have a deeper sense of self that cannot be reduced to our physical appearance. Our physical being exists, but it is only a small aspect of who we are.

We are also not our reason. Our thoughts are certainly more personal, more interior, and more nearly who we are than our appearance, but our way of thinking results in large measure from social conditioning. We are not our emotions. They, too, feel very personal, but since we can monitor them, they do not constitute the self. We experience our emotions, but cannot be reduced to them. We are not our egos. Ego in the Freudian sense is conditioned by the socially constructed superego and controlled by the biologically driven id. So deeper than physical being, reason, emotions, and ego lies the *real* self.

In the process of aging we let go of our physical being because we live through its transformation, but unless we are dualists, our physical self remains part of who we are. As we grow older we become aware of the limitations inherent in reason. Our society's rational system does not adequately explain what we know: our thoughts begin to break free. Aging also makes us more aware of the causes driving our emotions.

In chapter 6 we saw how Bernard's four stages in loving God respond to Job's suffering. We have also seen the inadequacies of taking any components of the self for the whole. Since the self is in relationship, we must explore where community fits in. Let us return to Bernard's four stages and substitute "community" each time we come to the term "God." We begin with self-love. Then we come to love others only instrumentally. We have seen how the self that regards the other as a means differs from the self that regards the other as intrinsically valuable. Finally, a long way down the road, we learn to love others for what they are in themselves. In the process we are transformed. We come to relate to others not as they seem to us but as they are in themselves. Finally we can *use* the self instead of focusing back on it. Now we can step into the self and become one with what is known, and thus we are expanded. We can take a further step if we can love ourselves for the roles we play in the being and well-being of others. Moving to this stage transforms the first.

When we love ourselves because we are important to the whole, the self we love is not the self that initially loved itself or even the self that loved the community for the sake of itself; it is the particular, historical self, replete with its unique memories and experiences. "One of the questions which inevitably arises in connection with rivers, estuaries, and the open sea is related to the fear of the loss of individual identity and almost 'drowning' in the ocean." This has been compared with "the opportunity of joining a larger life and relinquishing earlier feelings of being cut off from the 'mainstream of life.'"[6] We want to be part of the stream, but we also value the self with its unique history. The Bible repeatedly shows us individuals with their own family configurations and their own special characteristics. It is to these individual people, in their particular geographical and temporal setting, that God has been present, loving, and transformative. Our uniqueness is valued and taken up in the larger story that is God's endless courtship of humanity.

Let us now return to the Tree of the Knowledge of Good and Evil and try to understand the eating of the fruit. An interesting interpretation of the text is attributed by Arthur Waskow to his son David:

David—by that time ten years old—said, "I knew they would have to eat. The only way to find out what is 'good' is to do something bad. If you never do anything bad you never understand how to be good. If you never do anything bad you just *are*. You are not good and not bad. You just *are*. . . . There's only one kind of people who just *are*, and don't know anything about being good or bad. That's babies. Who would want to be a baby all his life?" I said, "But if you were a baby all your life, if you didn't grow up, you wouldn't get old. I guess you wouldn't die." But David insisted, "It isn't worth it. It's boring to be a baby all your life. I'd rather learn how to be good and bad and get old and die." "That's what the snake said." "He was right. He said knowing good and evil was being like God. That's right too." "But look how it all turned out!" "So it's just like now—people have to work hard, it hurts to have babies, all that stuff. So what? Would you rather be a baby all your life, so somebody would feed you all the time?" "But God told them not to eat!" "Yeah, but look how God makes such a thing about a Tree, they should be sure not to eat, and all that. Any kid would eat after that. It's almost like God teased them into eating. Maybe God wanted them to eat—but wanted them to think it was being bad to eat so then they'd have to think about being good and bad.'"[7]

We don't normally derive theological insights from a ten-year-old, but this interpretation has a simplicity and directness worth reflecting on. The fruit of the Tree does give knowledge and insight, but these are not the ultimate insights. Just as time is real but not ultimate, so the knowledge gained by eating the fruit is real but not ultimate. The ultimate knowledge does follow directly after the eating, but generally escapes our attention. The first "fruit" of the Tree is God's question to Adam and Eve, "Where are you?" That question could have been the beginning of their quest. Place, like time, may not be ultimate, but it provides a valuable way to explore identity. To fully understand place, Adam and Eve would have had to ask themselves how they got there, always a first step in *teshuvah*, the Hebrew word for repentance or returning. They would have speculated that where they came from was related to where they were going, a step toward the awareness of time.

In Jewish interpretations of the Tree story, knowledge is not the problem because it had been ordained prior to the Creation of the world that God would impart knowledge to humanity. The Torah, God's revelation to God's people, is said to have preexisted Creation and to have served as the blueprint for Creation. Even though people were always intended to have knowledge, we did not know, having eaten the fruit, how to relate that knowledge back to our primary relationship with God. Even now we may recognize that the river flowing through the Garden of Eden "divides and become four branches,"although we may not be able to trace the river back to its source.

While the story of the Tree is not about knowledge, it is not about disobedience either. Adam and Eve disobeyed, but *teshuvah* also is said to have existed before the Creation of the world. We must find our own way in the world, a way that might require testing and even disobedience, but God prepared a way back, *teshuvah*, before we were ever set into the Garden.

The curse on the serpent at the end of Genesis 3 is another invitation to know the self. The curse proclaims the otherness and enmity between the woman and the serpent but adds the cautionary, "they shall strike at your head, and you shall strike at their heel" (3:15). The woman cannot kill the serpent without risking herself and the serpent cannot strike without risking itself. Otherness is real and cannot be reduced to sameness, but neither is it destroyed without risk to the self.

The curse on the woman is the gift of her own procreativity. There will be pain in childbearing, as well as in child rearing, and even in a lifetime of love between the woman and the man, but pain is part of the difficult but essential quest for the self. The curse on the man is that he shall work. Work is, or can be, enacted love. The problem lies not in work itself but in the idea that the work is not rightfully *our* work. The difference between slavery and freedom is not that in one case we work and in the other we don't, but that free people's work expresses their own sense of value. All the so-called punishments are simply what is—the facts of life. But God is what is—"I Am what I Am" (Exod. 3:14)—and in whatever situation we find ourselves, in this place and this time, we can find God.

Adam and Eve were banished from the Garden and their way back was blocked by a cherub with a fiery sword. But their banishment was also a gift: only by setting out could they begin their quest for the self that would be their freely chosen way. Their journey, like ours, is an act of faith. Its goal will be appropriate to them and to us, but had we been told the end at the beginning, we would not have understood it because the goal is appropriate only for our transformed self. The end of the journey will, in one significant way, differ from the Edenic state. Eden did not result from freedom, and yet freedom above all is God's gift to creation. The end of the journey is freely chosen by those who complete it.

8 | *Leave-taking*

Through the biblical accounts of aging, we see that leave-taking serves important functions during the latter part of life. As the patriarchs and other characters age, they must take leave of their status, possessions, health, and loved ones. But in addition to loss, leave-taking always entails some gain: "Jacob's aging is irrevocable also, but the process is not merely one of decline and deterioration. He grows in dignity, stature, and significance as he becomes a patriarch."[1] Our most fundamental leave-taking is from an earlier concept of self.

The Israelites in the desert are also learning to say goodbye. If they are to become a nation of prophets and priests, they must develop their capacity to let go of what is known, familiar, and comfortable so they can move on to something new. But although taking leave, letting go, and saying goodbye are essential, they are not painless; in fact, they are wrenching. We suffer real and palpable losses; our gains, while no less real, are unexpected and we need time to assimilate them.

In committing ourselves to a historical religion we accept the reality of change and therefore the necessity of frequent good-byes. We may cast longing glances at the changeless world of the Platonic forms, but Plato's ideal is not the world of the Bible, which values time and the changes wrought through time. In such a world, we recognize and value the singular event, the unrepeatable context, and the unique, irreplaceable individual. We also find, in our particular time and place, and the family with whom we must finally make peace, all the raw materials we need for coming into God's presence. God meets us, not in some unspecified place in the midst of no activity, but in the particular place where we are doing what we are called upon to do. Our notion of a historical religion commits us to value the components of our personal history.

Valuing time entails the belief that time is real and that it serves as the medium for revelation, which in turn leads to the prophetic tradition and the call for social justice. People who were once enslaved and have been led to freedom know that change is possible and realize that their own history calls them to work for changes that lead to justice. Through such knowledge, the Children of Israel come to understand their being in terms of a task that must be completed. In a world of changeless forms, there can be no reform: things have always been as they are, and it is pointless and impossible to envision anything else. In a world that recognizes time and its processes, we hear the prophetic call and must respond to it.

The self we seek is not static, because the very process of searching for the self transforms it. The Israelites, for example, are transformed from a nation of slaves to a people of prophets and priests. We, too, seek to move from all that enslaves us to the freedom of being open to the spirit. Our process requires a life lived in friendship with time, a life in which we acknowledge change and accept loss. The mere words "accept loss" are, of course, far from the agony involved in the actual process. Losses take many forms and often manage to creep up on us undetected. We brace ourselves for a loss only to find that diminishment has occurred in an entirely different domain. "How it fools our sentinels and undermines our defenses, how careful we are to look for it in the wrong places, how it does not reveal itself until it is beyond redress, how vainly we search for it around us and find too late that it has occurred within us."[2]

What are all these losses? There is the loss of our fundamental values, which we cannot pass on. Isaac sends off his son, Jacob, and there is no record that he ever sees him again; we know only that Jacob returns to bury his father. As far as Isaac knows, his fundamental values would not be passed on. Isaac's values were born out of his agony on Mount Moriah, when his entire reality consisted of a knife aimed at his throat. His father's hand was stayed, and Isaac was not sacrificed. Somehow Isaac was able to wrest some value out of his pain-filled childhood. He attended the burial of *his* father. What anguished reflection allowed him to be capable of loving his wife? What enabled him to actually inhabit his faith? And what did it mean to him that he could not pass on his hard-won faith to his son?

Jacob saw his son Joseph move to greater and greater assimilation as an Egyptian. He knew that for seventeen years, while he had mourned his missing son as dead, Joseph had simply not bothered to inform him that he was alive. He knew the meanings of his grandsons' names, "the first-born Manasseh, meaning 'God has made me forget completely my hardship and my parental home.' And the second . . . Ephraim, meaning 'God has made me fertile in the land of my affliction'" (Gen. 41:51–52). We can easily imagine that Joseph rejected his parental home and that Jacob could not transmit his values to his favorite son. Jacob died before he could hear Joseph ask that his bones be carried out when the Children of Israel left Egypt.

The patriarchs may have hoped, but could not know, that the values central to their self-understanding would outlast their own lives. The pathos surrounding the separation of parents and children is expressed in God's complaint about the Children of Israel:

> Hear, O heavens, and give ear, O earth,
> For the Lord has spoken:
> "I reared children and brought them up—
> And they have rebelled against Me!
> An ox knows its owner,
> An ass its master's crib:
> Israel does not know,
> My people takes no thought."
>   (Isa. 1:2–3).

The text in Isaiah is mitigated by a promise of reconciliation in Malachi: "He shall reconcile fathers with sons and sons with their fathers" (Mal. 3:24). This promise, while not an immediate prospect, remains a long-range hope.

One generation passes and another emerges. This pattern would be a recapitulation without development, a tuneless air, were it not for love. We have postulated a world organized in terms of space, time, and beauty, which is the gift of love that underlies the relationship of Isaac to Jacob, Jacob to Joseph—indeed, of all the parents to their children and the children to their parents. Our world does not assure a specific outcome, but it does guarantee that whatever the outcome, the love will abide.

Our families are given to us. They become life-long arenas for working out the implications of particularity, of the many meanings of the time and place in which we have been set. Our friends, on the other hand, we choose, yet they often drop out of our lives.

Sometimes we simply lose them, perhaps through death, perhaps through the death of the values that formed the basis of our friendship. Such a loss is painful, but less so than discovering that we misjudged them and they have turned against us:

> It is not an enemy who reviles me
> —I could bear that;
> it is not my foe who vaunts himself against me
> —I could hide from him;
> but it is you, my equal,
> my companion, my friend;
> sweet was our fellowship;
> we walked together in God's house.
>
> (Ps. 55:13–15)

There are times when our losses overwhelm us. Even though we know intellectually that we carry within ourselves all that people have given us, we often feel very lonely. "I shall have to learn this lesson, too, and it will be the most difficult of all, 'oh God, to bear the suffering you have imposed on me and not just the suffering I have chosen for myself.'"[3] And that brings us what is perhaps the greatest loss of all, the loss of our self-image. We want to be open to what is asked of us, but we remain so only if what is asked happens to fit in with our plans. We can envision certain losses that could, in fact, be seen as gains. If we lose our job or our status, we can do so with such dignity that we will grow in self-respect and gain in the eyes of those who matter to us. But our actual losses have little to do with our self-dramatizing agenda. "Self-knowledge destroys his opinion of himself, his conceit, his assumptions, the world that he had constructed for himself."[4] Our deepest losses frequently occur in areas so central that we do not even reflect on them. This is who we are, how can it be otherwise? Discovering that our basic sense of ourselves is vulnerable, or is under siege, or has even been destroyed is to lose our bearings and be thrust into the desert.

The Israelites' most momentous experience of leave-taking occurred at the Exodus from Egypt into the desert. The Israelites had to say goodbye to a culture, a way of life, a series of landmarks, and a way of viewing the world. Their goodbye was a prerequisite for entering into a new way of life. That they were leaving servitude should, we might think, have mitigated the pain of their entry into the desert. But the Hebrew scriptures suggest that we are all in servitude although we may not consciously be able to recognize and name our taskmasters. Our current way of life may be painful, even hateful, but we often cannot envision an alternative. What is hard for us was no less difficult for the Children of Israel. They had to struggle to reach the point of readiness to leave Egypt, and we must struggle if we are to leave our current way of life. Whatever is deeply familiar, wherever we have lived out our lives, is, however painful, home. Home can be dysfunctional, but it is home. We marvel that the Children of Israel could have longed for the fleshpots of Egypt, but we do no less when we feel nostalgia for the very settings that enslave us. And the Children of Israel did go off into the desert.

The desert is the place where we cannot hide from ourselves, where our roles and our normal ways of life are cast aside. Time spent in the desert can be an experience of radical loss, and if that were the whole story, the desert would hold no attraction for us. But time in the desert can also be understood as a time of growing intimacy with God. Then we feel compensated for the losses we suffer in the wilderness.

Our growing intimacy with God actually requires leave-taking because to achieve it we must shed everything that is less than true. We live with appearance instead of reality; we live with false notions of who we are and what we can have. What we think we have is not truly ours to possess, to control, or to shape. God gives us the gift of freedom and we, in God's image, must bequeath freedom to our children. We cannot mold them without distorting them or ourselves. What Isaac values but cannot bequeath, what Jacob finally achieves but cannot pass on, is nothing other than the reality of God's presence. God's presence is not second-hand, it simply cannot be passed on. It is always new and always newly experienced.

We feel deeply the loss of those who have dropped out of our lives, until we understand that people cannot be grasped, possessed, or held fast. The losses occur and recur as we struggle to remain open to intimacy and love.

Our self-image needs honest scrutiny. Discovering our weaknesses, vulnerabilities, inconsistencies, pettinesses, and flaws would be overwhelming and ultimately destructive were we not aware of our growing intimacy with God. The desert without God would be desolate. But we undergo this process of stripping away all that protected and sheltered us in the knowledge that God led us into the desert and sustained and sheltered us there.

Our growing intimacy with God transforms leave-taking by

allowing us to recognize that parting does not require absolute loss. We carry people with us—or, those aspects of them that we have incorporated into ourselves. We are the artifact of all who have come into our lives by loving us, teaching us, interacting with us. They cannot mold us any more than we can mold our children, but they can help us discover and realize who we could become. We also remember people. Just as God has numbered all our tears and not allowed our experiences to be forgotten, we hold in sacred memory the people who belong to our lives. We love people as opening us up to God. Since God is ever-present, there is a sense in which even those we lose remain with us. In recognizing our losses we are forced to realize that we are ephemeral. Left to ourselves we cannot prevent any loss from being final. But while our sojourn in the desert is a time of stripping down and taking away, it also leads to a growing intimacy with God, which in turn engenders trust. What we cannot preserve, hold, or remember is nonetheless lifted up and cherished by God. All is in God's hands. In Giordano Bruno's words, "Out of this universe you cannot fall," so nothing, nothing is ever lost.

In the desert God leads the Children of Israel with a pillar of cloud by day and a pillar of fire by night. Originally the cloud pillar protects the Israelites from the pursuing Egyptians by standing between the two peoples: "Thus there was the cloud with the darkness, and it cast a spell upon the night, so that the one could not come near the other all through the night" (Exod. 14:20). But after the Egyptians no longer represent a threat, the pillar of cloud continues to tell the Israelites when and when not to set out on their various journeys. What does it mean to be led by a pillar of cloud? It means that God's direction is ultimately mysterious. The cloud (so like the medieval "cloud of unknowing") becomes a symbol for the mystery of being led by God. The cloud leads by day, the pillar of fire by night. While we tend, in the light of day, to trust our own discernment, the cloud reminds us that there is much we cannot perceive. At night when our courage fails us, the pillar of fire assures us that even in the darkness there is light. In both day and night God appears as "other," other than our daytime confidence or our nighttime terror. Here we are taking leave of our own plans and judgments in order to enter into the mystery and trust required for following God's way.

Observing the Sabbath is another form of taking leave. The practice of the Sabbath is instituted in the desert with the gathering of the manna:

And the Lord said to Moses, "I will rain down bread for you from the sky, and the people shall go out and gather each day that day's portion—that I may thus test them, to see whether they will follow My instructions or not. But on the sixth day, when they prepare what they have brought in, it shall prove to be double the amount they gather each day.". . . On the sixth day they gathered double the amount of food, two *omers* for each; and when all the chieftains of the assembly came and told Moses, he said to them, "This is what the Lord meant: Tomorrow is a day of rest, a holy Sabbath of the Lord. Bake what you would bake and boil what you would boil; and all that is left put aside to be kept until morning.". . . Then Moses said, "Eat it today, for today is the Sabbath of the Lord; you will not find it today on the plain. Six days you shall gather it; on the seventh day, the Sabbath, there will be none.". . . "Mark that the Lord has given you the Sabbath; therefore He gives you two days' food on the sixth day. Let everyone remain where he is: let no man leave his place on the seventh day." So the people remained inactive on the seventh day. (Exod. 16:4–30)

During six days of the week personal efforts determine wellbeing. But on the seventh the Children of Israel must forego effort and take the world as it is, not as it is for them. The weekly institution of the Sabbath trains the Israelites to develop trust that the world can indeed support their needs. Sabbath is not an institution of passivity or quietism. Never far from the Israelites' consciousness is the sense that there is a task they must be doing: "The day is short; the task is great; the workmen are lazy; the reward is great, and the Master is insistent." But while the Children of Israel must work and must contribute, their lives do not, finally, depend upon their own efforts. "You are not called to complete the work, yet you are not free to evade it."[5] So each week they learn that they can rest in a world that is sufficient to sustain them and then, refreshed, go out once again to make their contribution. So much of what we experience is the world as it is to us, as it meets our needs or thwarts our efforts. The Sabbath reminds us that the world is prior to and more than the product of our shaping. Once a week we recognize this more and rest in it.

The weekly institution of the Sabbath instills in us some confidence in the process of giving up control. We discover that just because *we* don't control the world, that does not mean that the world is uncontrolled. Similarly, our experience of separation allows us to gain some confidence in the process of leave-taking. Separation is frequently creative. As we focus on the ways in which separation has led us to growth, we gain confidence in the process—from the first separation that led to our independent being to the separations we experience as we move to embrace larger communities throughout childhood and young adulthood. We live out in our own lives that first separation, which initiated the entire quest for the self: "Go forth from your native land and from your father's house to the land that I will show you" (Gen. 12:1).

Our song, our narrative, our journey, can be construed as music unfolding over time, or as plot developing over time, or as space unfolding over time. The music, the plot, the space, represent the content: they are all the things we have seen, experienced, reflected upon, and interacted with.

The biblical view of time is central to our concept of leave-taking. The concept cannot exist without our capacity to remember. Nor can there be a future without our capacity to envision. Beginnings and futures are both shaped by an awareness of the beginning and development of our own song within the context of the larger song of our people. In the process, time has become our companion and friend as we explore its three dimensions and unite them into one song.

Our final leave-taking is from the very stories and songs that have nourished us in our quest. As much as we have learned from the story of our ancestors, we must let go of all we have used to help us get at the self. That may mean letting go of the formal story and the other characters. The desert *is* the desert, and no landmark can accompany us here. For the same reasons that Isaac and Jacob could not bequeath their central values to their offspring, we cannot inherit ours from the biblical stories. Our central value is God's presence, which can never be passed on—it is always new and always newly experienced. From the biblical stories we can inherit expectations, goals, and direction. But finally we must experience our own Exodus, our own sojourn in the desert, and be open to God's transformative presence.

9 | *Awakening*

We began with a quest, an all-engrossing search for the self, that took us through memory, the desert, the process of aging and facing death, and the inevitable leave-takings that constitute a part of life. When we have reflected on our past, faced our fears and vulnerabilities, and accepted the aging process as well as the many losses we sustain throughout life, to what do we awaken?

When we first awaken, we ask, "Where am I?" The answer is, "Here, in this place where you have been set down." We awaken from this marvelous quest to our own daily world. We have discovered that time is essential to a historical religion, and that time's irreversibility leads to uniqueness, particularity, and individuality. We are not set down somewhere, somehow, in some time. We are set down in a particular geographical location, in a particular family, and in our own place within that family, that history, and that setting. We do not return to Eden. Eden is the harbor from which we set sail, not the harbor in which we drop anchor. We do not awaken to a transformed world, but because we have been transformed, we find our daily world new. We awaken to find the extraordinary in the ordinary.

Our second question is, "Who am I?" In searching for a response, we have expended much effort in rejecting easy answers: we are *not* our appearance, our cognitive ability, our emotions, or our ego. At the same time, we have taken steps toward understanding the self, such as claiming and restructuring our memory and acknowledging and accepting the fears that cut us off from aspects of our self. In facing our fears, we recognize how very long we have spent projecting what we feared onto the outer world. We also projected our hopes. Rarely did we look within and claim what was there all along.

Stirring up memory reminded us of the discomfort and unease that set us off on our quest in the first place. But where is the pain, the evil? It is still here, where we put it aside as we set off to uncover our deepest sense of self. The pain and evil remain, but they are encapsulated. Evil is no longer a threat. Just as we have learned not to throw out part of our self, but to determine its role in the larger whole, so we learn that the evil and pain also have a role to play in the larger whole. There can be no radical otherness.

Where are we? Who are we? And in what condition do we find ourselves? The formative story spelled out in the Bible is that of a movement from slavery to freedom. As we trace the analogous journey in our own lives, we sense a similar movement toward freedom. Freedom is not merely the absence of constraints; positively understood, it is our creative capacity to envision and enact new worlds. The journey to freedom presupposes the journey to self-understanding because freedom is, as Baruch Spinoza defines it, "acting from the necessity of our own nature." We are no longer surprised to find "freedom" and "necessity" within the same definition: these supposed opposites are part of a unified whole.

We began our examination with Genesis. Comparable to the Edenic state is our own childhood. We tend to look back on our childhood as a time of freedom, but that view represents nostalgia far removed from the truth. We are not free when we are children—freedom demands consciousness and a vision of alternatives. Just as there is no freedom in Eden, so there is no freedom in childhood.

We found that our consciousness is shaped musically, which explains the priority of sound over sight and time over space. And within the structure of music we found improvisation, our first representation of freedom. Applying our shared musical heritage, we maintain the basic structure and form of a given theme and still find room to improvise and make it uniquely our own. The immediate value of such improvisation is a renewal and a revivification of our world. The same events now sound more fully, resonate more richly, and uncover hidden harmonies.

Essential to freedom is our capacity to distinguish between appearance and reality. Platonists and the Bible draw this distinction in radically different ways, but despite their differences, they agree that the world is more than it seems to be. The quest for that more—the search for the underlying reality—is essential for gaining freedom. If our vision is reduced only to what appears to us, we are robbed of the possibility to interpret. Our world would be constricted, and we would no longer be free.

Memory plays a twofold role in freedom. In its negative use, it frees us from the unresolved issues of the past. Freedom is freedom to act, not to react. Just as the Israelites had to deal not only with physical servitude but with the Egyptian view of them as slaves, so we must recover, review, and resolve others' views of ourselves that we have internalized. The negative use of memory may be difficult and even painful, but it is productive. Positively, memory provides a way of reentering into times of intimacy and trust with God, not simply for nostalgic reasons but to allow us to experience a Presence that once was.

When we explored the desert experience, we found that at its core is—not accidentally—revelation. If we wish to arrive at what is genuinely new and revelatory, we must be willing to enter the chaos and abyss of rejected order and structure. Structure breeds security, but revelation requires that we go beyond security to what is new, what lies outside our usual ways of thinking.

That we move to greater and greater freedom even as our body deteriorates suggests that freedom is far more than the removal of physical constraints. The more deeply we live and reflect upon our experiences, the more clearly we see that much of our energy has been exerted on appearance, not reality, and that much of our concern has been wasted in seeking the approval of those who cannot serve as a standard. Our need for approval dissipates, our goals change, and we get clearer about what is real. The self, through all this, does not disappear, it is transformed. Social construction of the self diminishes, but something deeper and more ultimate than society remains. The self comes to trust this more essential definition and endures the paring away of all that is less than true. Genuine loss is entailed in this paring, but it is felt to be meaningful loss. In our genuine freedom we return to our daily world with energy and with delight for the work to be done. Our joy is expansive, so the happiness of others expands us: we are connected to other people in the world.

Self occurs in context, that is, the time and place in which we are set down and the particular people who come into our lives. But the most important context is Presence. Presence transforms a horde of fleeing slaves into a nation of prophets and priests. It transforms our work from drudgery into occasions of sacrament by lifting up moments in time, turning the ephemeral into the eternal. It led the Children of Israel on their journey in the wilderness, and it leads us on our quest for the self. But just what is Presence, how can we recognize it, and how can we distinguish it from absence?

Trying to characterize Presence enmeshes us in contradiction. If Presence is what leads the Israelites to continue their journey and also tells them to stop, then it is not merely peace, it is peace combined with restlessness. We may emphasize Presence as a spur to action or as a source of homecoming and quiet, but we cannot define it this way if restlessness and peace contradict one another.

Presence is not simply healing, it is frequently wounding. It satisfies all longings while it creates a longing that cannot be satisfied. As we see the contradictions piling up, we begin to understand experientially what the coincidence of opposites is all about. We first encountered the coincidence of opposites when we pondered whether God created darkness or darkness represented the absence of light. We kept coming across the notion as we saw the breakdown of dualisms and sensed an underlying unity. But experientially the concept remained abstract, and the abstract is never part of our world. Once we admit something to our world, we see it as particular and concrete. So in a real sense, we knew we had not understood the coincidence of opposites because we could not move beyond abstract, cognitive descriptions. And yet we are drawn to the realization that nothing less than the coincidence of opposites will allow us to talk about Presence. Presence is not abstract, it is experienced by particular people at particular times in definite places. It is this concrete experience of Presence that is central to the whole notion of self and central to the experience of the Israelites. "The reality of the presence of God stands at the center of biblical faith. . . . It is the distinctiveness of the Hebraic theology of presence rather than the ideology of the covenant which provides a key to understanding the Bible."[1] Finally, the coincidence of opposites becomes not something we have only heard, thought, or reasoned about, but something we experience and *know*.

In our quest for freedom we explored Spinoza's definition that freedom is acting from the necessity of our own nature. Here again we see the coincidence of opposites: Doesn't freedom imply the absence of all necessity? We think of people whose unchanging behavior is dismissed with the thought "that's just their nature," implying an inevitability and determinism that seems to contradict freedom. But if we look beyond the socially constructed self of appearance to the essential nature of self, we see that our essential nature is the source of our freedom. It is instructive that Dante's words, "In His will is our peace," appear in the *Paradiso*. At an earlier stage in our development, when we do not identify with the essential nature of self, the will of God seems external to us and constricting of our own will. The souls in Dante's paradise have come to know that God's will accords with their own deepest nature, so they can experience peace in God's will and not chafe against it.

Let us approach the coincidence of opposites from a related perspective. We have long known that there is pain in love but have somehow avoided reflecting on our experience. We have tended to regard the inevitable conjunction of love and pain as "paradoxical." But now we can see that paradox itself points to the deeper reality of the coincidence of opposites. How right that love, which is another name for God, should come to us in two guises: joy, which Spinoza defines as expansion of the self to a greater perfection, and pain, which he defines as movement from a greater to a lesser perfection.

How right that we should search for a love that does not diminish the self, a love that is without pain. Spinoza observes that

> happiness or unhappiness is made wholly to depend on the quality of the object which we love. When a thing is not loved, no quarrels will arise concerning it—no sadness will be felt if it perishes—no envy if it is possessed by another—no fear, no hatred, in short no disturbances of the mind. All these arise from the love of what is perishable, such as the objects already mentioned. But love toward a thing eternal and infinite feeds the mind wholly with joy, and is itself unmingled with any sadness, wherefore it is greatly to be desired and sought for with all our strength.[2]

The Roman Stoics sought freedom and believed that pain represented a life of slavery. In order to attain true freedom, the Stoics turned inward and tried to remain untouched by the things of this world. This view, which requires an emotional withdrawal from the world, reemerges in medieval Christianity and in some forms of Buddhism, but it is not the biblical view. The Bible promises freedom—not freedom from pain, but freedom to seek meaning and value. The stoics of every age are correct—if we have no love we will have no disturbances of mind—but the Bible enjoins us to "love your neighbor as yourself" (Lev. 19:18). The answer that we are to love "a thing eternal and infinite" addresses only the biblical injunction to "love the Lord your God with all your heart and with all your soul and with all your might" (Deut. 6:5) and not "to love your neighbor as yourself." Nor can we accept Augustine's answer that we are to love our finite neighbor *in* God: while God remains eternal, our finite neighbor is all too mortal. Our love for God will give meaning to our loss, but it will not eliminate our pain and suffering. The Bible does not promise freedom from suffering but freedom to find meaning in and through suffering. Those closest to God frequently suffer the most because they are deeply compassionate and are open to experience the full pain of injustice. Their capacity to love increases their experience of pain, and so they live out the coincidence of opposites.

The head and the heart form another coincidence of opposites. We saw earlier that the self does not know God, even while we understand the terms *self* and *God* in a very limited way. The more we know about God, the more we know about the self, and the more we know about the self, the more we know about God. The Bible does not portray abstract, impersonal knowledge: knowledge transforms and incorporates the whole person. It transforms the knower because of the union that occurs between the knower and the known. This use of the verb "to know" is exemplified by the passage, "Now the man knew his wife Eve, and she conceived and bore Cain" (Gen. 4:1), which demonstrates that knowledge is transformative and fruitful. Here, to know (head) and to love (heart) are synonymous.

The self that can love a thing eternal and infinite is not the one that began the quest but the one that has journeyed through.

If Presence both heals and wounds, brings peace and unease, both satisfies and arouses desire, how do we recognize the experience of Presence and how does it differ from the experience of absence? Initially the children of Israel thought Presence could guarantee a desired outcome:

> For our sons are like saplings,
>> well-tended in their youth;
>> our daughters are like cornerstones
>> trimmed to give shape to a palace.
> Our storehouses are full,

> supplying produce of all kinds;
> our flocks number thousands,
> even myriads, in our fields;
> our cattle are well cared for.
> There is no breaching and no sortie,
> and no wailing in our streets.
> Happy the people who have it so;
> happy the people whose God is the Lord.
>
> (Ps. 144:12–15)

But Presence neither guarantees a desired outcome nor prevents a feared one. Presence is consistent with euphoria and elation, but also with grief and mourning. Presence is real and therefore makes a profound difference, but the difference is one of meaning rather than outcome. Without Presence, we understand all that occurs to be chance, luck, or fate; with Presence, all that occurs opens us to relatedness and meaning. There is much about Presence that is also true of love: love does not guarantee a desired outcome or prevent a feared one, but it does guarantee its own abidingness. Presence, too, guarantees its abidingness:

> Where can I escape from your spirit?
> Where can I flee from Your presence?
> If I ascend to heaven, You are there;
> if I descend to Sheol, You are there too.
> If I take wing with the dawn
> to come to rest on the western horizon,
> even there Your hand will be guiding me,
> Your right hand will be holding me fast.
>
> (Ps. 139:7–10)

Is there any possibility of absence? If God is what is—"I Am," or reality—then we can have only absence of attention, not absence of Presence. And we do, indeed, want to identify reality with God's presence—reality, *not* appearance. We have lived too long in the world of appearance—how things seem to us—but now and then reality breaks through to transform us and our perception of the world. If we understand that Presence is always given and it is only our attention that is sometimes absent, then we see that we could live perpetually in the Presence. The Israelites spent all of their time in the desert after the revelation at Sinai educating themselves for remaining open to Presence amid daily life. We need not be particularly perceptive or spiritually open to be aware of Presence when the shofar sound grows louder, the sky darkens, and the thunder rolls. Being aware becomes

more difficult in the many years after Sinai, and still more difficult when the Children of Israel leave the desert and settle in the
land of Canaan. There are always some amid the people who
remain attentive and seek to remind the others that a pillar of
cloud still leads them. Often they are not heard, or heard only in
retrospect, "Yes they were right." But the attentive ones stir a
memory in the rest of the people:

> Take us back, O Lord, to Yourself,
>   And let us come back;
>   Renew our days as of old!
>   (Lam. 5:22)

Those who stay open and attentive differ from those who do
not in that they keep singing their song. The song begins with the
distinction between appearance and reality, a distinction not of
opposition but of part to whole. The attentive refuse to accept the
part as the whole, refuse to settle for the appearance. Their refusal
to close off their possibilities too soon leaves them open to perceive when others have ceased to attend. Attention leads to God.
The attentive cherish their memories, rehearse what God has
done in days of yore, and make current the Presence that nourished them in the past. Memory allows them to make the past
present and effective now.

The attentive are never far from the desert. They acknowledge
and claim their terrifying memories, transformed now by the
Presence of God; they claim their physical vulnerabilities and the
anger and aggression they have suffered and caused; they attend
to their unnameable fears and to the creativity that resides within
all these trials. They have made peace with time and the transformations that time brings through aging. They have "stepped
into" the self so that it no longer stands in front of them, obscur-
ing all they wish to see. They use the self rather than focus on it
and so are open to reality. Finally, the attentive have gained sufficient trust to release and give—rather than having wrenched
away and stolen—all that must be let go. Nothing can block their
awareness of Presence.

We had thought that our quest would result in a new understanding of the self. What has emerged instead is an openness to
Presence. The self is a self in relationship—the relationship to
Presence. All the false selves we moved beyond in our quest—
appearance, reason, emotions, ego—are obstructions to Presence.

We blocked our own attentiveness and distracted ourself from reality.

"Because biblical people knew God, they knew the self. That was their principle of coherence. From the knowledge of God all else flowed."[3] But knowledge is not cognitive, abstract knowledge. For biblical people knowledge is relatedness. We may live in a different time, a different part of the world, a different intellectual climate, but the insight of biblical people remains true. When we know God, then and only then will we know the self.

Notes

Quotations from the Hebrew scriptures are drawn primarily from the 1967 translation by the Jewish Publication Society.

1. Genesis

1. Walter Kaufmann, *Time Is an Artist* (New York: Reader's Digest Press, 1978), 37.
2. Ernesto Galarza, "Could Be," in *Kodachromes in Rhyme* (Notre Dame: University of Notre Dame Press, 1982), 53.

2. Song

1. John Grinder and Richard Bandler, *The Structure of Magic*, vol. 2 (Palo Alto, Calif.: Science and Behavior Books, 1976), 4, 8–9.
2. Samuel Terrien, *The Elusive Presence* (San Francisco: Harper and Row, 1978), 127–28.
3. Ibid., 202.
4. Will Herberg, "The Fundamental Outlook of Hebraic Religion," in *The Ways of Religion*, ed. Roger Eastman (San Francisco : Harper and Row, 1975), 287.
5. Stephen Crites, "The Narrative Quality of Experience," *Journal of the American Academy of Religion* 39 (1971): 291–311.
6. Mortimer Cass, "A Note on Music," in *Creativity*, ed. Silvano Arieti (New York: Basic Books, 1976), 236–37.
7. Robert Grudin, *The Grace of Great Things* (New York: Ticknor and Fields, 1990), 58–59.
8. T. S. Eliot, *Four Quartets* (New York: Harcourt, Brace, 1943), 27.
9. Oliver Sacks, *The Man Who Mistook His Wife for a Hat* (New York: Harper and Row, 1987), 147; Sacks, *Migraine* (Berkeley: University of California Press, 1985), 165; Sacks, *Awakenings*, new ed. (New York: E. P. Dutton, 1983), 99.

10. Oliver Sacks, *A Leg to Stand On* (New York: Harper and Row, 1984), 119.
11. Grudin, *Grace*, 7.
12. Martin Buber, *I and Thou*, trans. Walter Kaufmann (New York: Charles Scribner's Sons, 1970), 60.

3. Appearance

1. William Blake, *The Poetical Works*, ed. William Michael Rossetti (London: G. Bell, 1874), 164.
2. Kaufmann, *Time Is an Artist*, 40.
3. Ibid., 57.
4. *Ethics of the Fathers*, 2:21, trans. Philip Birnbaum, in *Daily Prayer Book* (New York: Hebrew Publishing Co., 1949), 492.
5. *The Passover Haggadah*, trans. Philip Birnbaum (New York: Hebrew Publishing Co., 1953), 47.

4. Memory

1. Kathleen Fischer, *Winter Grace* (New York: Paulist Press, 1985), 35, 38.
2. Jeanne Barker-Nunn, "Telling the Mother's Story: History and Connection in the Autobiographies of Maxine Hong Kingston and Kim Chernin," *Women's Studies* 14 (1987): 57.
3. Robert Grudin, *Time and the Art of Living* (New York: Ticknor and Fields, 1982), 33.
4. Attributed to John Cage and others.
5. Walter Kaufmann, *Man's Lot* (New York: Reader's Digest Press, 1978), 57.
6. Sacks, *The Man*, 23, quoting Luis Buñuel.
7. Ibid., 34.
8. Ibid., 38.
9. Grudin, *Time*, 13.
10. Ibid., 114.
11. Stanley Keleman, *Living Your Dying* (New York: Random House, 1974), 90–91.
12. Ibid., 89.
13. Grudin, *Time*, 43.
14. Elie Wiesel, *Souls on Fire* (New York: Random House, 1972), 226.
15. Grudin, *Grace*, 19–20.
16. Arthur R. Gold, "Exodus as Autobiography," *Commentary*, May 1967: 47.

5. Desert

1. Gold, "Exodus as Autobiography," 48.

2. Quoted in Uwe George, *In the Deserts of This Earth* (New York: Harcourt Brace Jovanovich, 1979), 6.

3. Oliver Sacks, "Neurology and the Soul," *New York Review of Books*, November 22, 1990: 46.

4. George, *Deserts*, 175–76.

5. Walter Kaufmann, introduction to Buber, *I and Thou*, 25–26.

6. Buber, *I and Thou*, 59.

7. Kathleen Fischer, *Women at the Well* (New York: Paulist Press, 1988), 59.

8. Grudin, *Grace*, 59.

6. Aging

1. John S. Dunne, *The Way of All the Earth: Experiments in Truth and Religion* (New York: Macmillan, 1972; rpt., Notre Dame: University of Notre Dame Press, 1978), 31–32.

2. Kaufmann, *Man's Lot*, 124.

3. Evelyn Eaton Whitehead and James D. Whitehead, *Christian Life Patterns* (Garden City, N.Y. : Doubleday, 1982), 184.

4. Buber, *I and Thou*, 108.

5. Mishnah 2: Ta'anith 2:2, in *The Mishnah*, tr. Herbert Danby (Oxford: Oxford University Press, 1933), 196.

6. May Sarton, *After the Stroke* (New York: Norton, 1988), 124–25.

7. *Ethics of the Fathers*, 1:14, trans. Joseph H. Hertz, in *The Authorised Daily Prayer Book*, rev. ed. (New York: Bloch Publishing Co., 1957), 625.

8. John S. Dunne, *The Homing Spirit* (New York: Crossroad, 1987), 84.

9. Thomas Merton, *The Sign of Jonas* (Garden City, N.Y.: Doubleday, 1956), 230.

10. Grudin, *Time*, 118.

11. Fischer, *Winter Grace*, 4.

12. Paul Tournier, *Learn to Grow Old* (San Francisco: Harper and Row, 1983), 179.

13. Kaufmann, *Man's Lot*, 61, 64.

14. Elisabeth Kübler-Ross, *On Death and Dying* (New York: Macmillan, 1969), 258–59.

15. Abraham Joshua Heschel, "Death as Homecoming," in *Jewish Reflections on Death*, ed. Jack Riemer (New York: Schocken Books, 1974), 62, 73.

7. Quest for the Self

1. Frederick Franck, *The Buddha Eye* (New York: Crossroad, 1982), 28.
2. Maurice Maeterlinck, *Death* (New York: Arno Press, 1977), 105.
3. Heschel, "Death as Homecoming," 73.
4. Joanna Field, *An Experiment in Leisure* (Los Angeles: Jeremy P. Tarcher, 1987), 45, 147; Kaufmann, *Man's Lot*, 56.
5. William Johnston, *Being in Love* (San Francisco: Harper and Row, 1989), 69.
6. Murray Cox and Alice Theilgaard, *Mutative Metaphors in Psychotherapy* (London: Tavistock, 1987), 108.
7. Arthur I. Waskow, *Godwrestling* (New York: Schocken Books, 1978), 47.

8. Leave-taking

1. Kaufmann, *Time*, 38.
2. Grudin, *Time*, 6.
3. Etty Hillesum, *An Interrupted Life* (New York: Washington Square Press, 1981), 231.
4. Kaufmann, *Man's Lot*, 56.
5. *Ethics of the Fathers*, 2:20, 2:21, trans. Birnbaum, in *Daily Prayer Book*, 492.

9. Awakening

1. Terrien, *The Elusive Presence*, xxvii–xxviii.
2. Baruch Spinoza, *Ethics, Preceded by "On the Improvement of the Understanding,"* ed. James Gutmann (New York: Hafner, 1955), 5.
3. Robert S. Bilheimer, *A Spirituality for the Long Haul* (Philadelphia: Fortress Press, 1984), 19.

Index